Flint Castle

The story of Edward I's first Welsh castle

Vicky Perfect

Copyright © 2012 Vicky Perfect c/o **Alyn Books** Ltd, The Nook, Pentre Road, Cilcain, Mold, Flintshire CH7 5PD.

ISBN 978-0-9559625-7-8

Modern photography: Jo Danson, Lorna Jenner, Vicky Perfect, Carl Rogers, Flintshire County Council

Bird photography: Simon Booth, Steve Jones

Black and white drawings: Tim Johnson, Bill Smuts, Michael Roberts

Printed by: Ashford Press

With special thanks to Lorna Jenner for all her help and advice in the compilation of the book, Carl Rogers for his photographic help, Bill Smuts, Tim Johnson and Michael Roberts for the use of their drawings, Bill and Carl for their design work and finally Alyn Books who had enough faith in my research to have the book printed.

Cover images: Flint Castle by Chris Hull

To historian Henry Taylor whose writing about Flint inspired me to write this book, although I never had the pleasure of meeting him.

Henry Taylor

HOUSE OF COMMONS
LONDON SWIA OAA

Our Ref: DH/HR.misc.p

1st October 2010

I am really excited about this new book from Vicky Perfect, and I am particularly pleased that I have been asked to write the foreword.

The history of Flint Castle is part of the life-blood of Flint. Ever since the start of the Castle building in 1277 by Edward I, through to such momentous events as the deposing of Richard II or the shelling in the English Civil War, Flint Castle has played a part in the life of the Town and the nation as a whole.

This book tells the story of the Castle and town from its Roman origins to medieval times, through to the modern icon it remains today. I live in the Town and I am looking forward to learning more about the Castle, the Dock and its history.

I know everyone who picks this book up will find it equally fascinating. Thank you for writing it Vicky and good luck!

David Hanson MP
Delyn

Contents

Foreword

Why anyone becomes interested in history can be a mystery to some people. Why would anyone want to delve into the past? To many this sounds a dull pastime. Some find current events more interesting, but to understand today and how we got to this stage, you sometimes need to look back into the past to get a better understanding of things.

My interest in history did not happen in school. I was more interested in music and where the Beatles or Rolling Stones were in the charts, which was the norm for my generation. I was 'a child of the Sixties', flower power, the Beatles, tuning in and dropping out, although personally I didn't drop out.

I became interested in history when a profound event took place in my personal life. In 1974 my mother, Prudence Aldridge, died of cancer when I was twenty five; I firstly felt an overwhelming sense of grief, a profound loss, and that loss developed into a curiosity about her life. I realised that I knew very little of my mother's personal life, other than she was mother to me and my three brothers and four sisters and there it was now over. All the questions about her schooling, her growing up, what made her tick could never be answered by her; there was so much to learn and the one person I wanted to ask these questions to was no longer around to answer them.

This was the starting point into a love of history that still exists today. How did it change from curiosity about my mother's life, to a profound passion for all things historical? When I had my first daughter, Michelle, on June 23rd 1975, it was a good summer, nice and warm, the type of weather that takes you out of doors for a walk with a new pram and new baby. I found myself wandering to Flint Castle, sitting there on the North East wall of the castle looking out to Parkgate, watching as a large barge was going up the river Dee. It was so peaceful, a really pleasurable experience. I started thinking to myself, who built this castle and why did they build it here?

I had visited the castle for as long as I can remember, since I was a young girl, but on this day some twenty-six years later a curiosity about this old building started to form. It was time to find out some local history I thought, and I set off for the local library and that was the start of my journey into history.

However, it was not until I read Henry Taylor's Historic Notices, written in 1883, that I became enlightened so to speak. Henry in the preface of his book says,

That the kindred spirit who may hereafter aim to write a more extensive and complete History of Flint may not turn to these pages altogether in vain

To someone who is embarking on local history like myself those remarks were so understated, because reading his Historic Notices opened up a whole new world of discovery into the town's past. All sorts can be gleaned from his book and I advise anyone who is embarking on a study of Flint to seek this book out in the library and read it before beginning your own studies, for it is an excellent starting point.

I have much to thank Henry Taylor for and I dedicate this small contribution to him and my totally supportive family, my husband Eddie, and daughters Michelle and Adele.

I hope this book will spark an interest in and increase your knowledge about Flint Castle and help you to understand why it has become such a passion of mine.

Vicky Perfect

Chapter 1

Early Settlements

The area that later became known as Flint has a long and fascinating history. It was rich in natural resources and valued from its earliest beginnings.

The Romans were the first to recognise its value and developed two settlements. The first was to the west of where Flint Castle now stands. Roman tiles were found here when the site was excavated to build the foundations of the United Alkali Works, around 1850.

The second settlement, about a mile south-east of the present town at what is now Oakenholt, was more important, built for the purpose of lead smelting. The smelting area was known as Pentre-Ffwrn-Dan 'the vill of the burning furnace'. It would undoubtedly have been a very hot and unpleasant place to work. The workers lived at the nearby settlement known as Atis Cross (now Croes Atti). The Romans also established a port for the transportation of the pigs of smelted lead to Deva (Chester).

Roderic the Great was the first recorded person to mention the area in 870. Henry Taylor refers to this in his Historic Notices of Flint in 1883.

In 870 Roderic the Great, King of Wales, made a division of his dominions amongst his three sons, and ordained that if any quarrel should arise between the Princes of North Wales and Powys a meeting should be held at Morfa-Rhianedd*, on the banks of the Dee, where the Prince of South Wales was to determine the controversy.[1]

*Morfa Rhianedd later became known as Oakenholt

Roderic the Great must have recognised the area's strategic position in choosing it as the meeting point. It had good access by sea, which was really important in those days.

The area has two mentions in the Domesday Book. The settlement that became Flint was then a merely a small hamlet known as Raddington, which was held by the Earl of Chester, Hugh Lupus, nephew to William the

Right: Roman soldier

Conquerer. He was an ancestor of the Duke of Westminster and his tomb can be seen in Chester Cathedral.

Atis Cross, which gave its name to the Hundred (an administrative area like Flintshire is today) in which the present town of Flint lies, is also mentioned in the Domesday Book, described as:

> *A small Hamlet under the diocese of Northop, being held by Earl Hugh paying geld on one hide, with room for one plough team.[2]*

(*A plough team consisted of a team of six oxen and one cart; a hide was as much land as could be measured by an ox-hide cut into thin strips, known as thongs. It was not an exact quantity, roughly around 120 acres, and it varied in importance depending on the vill it referred to.*)

The inclusion of a water mill to grind the corn, near to St. David's Church (known locally as Danny Shurwin's), made the Atis Cross area even more valuable.

However, the fumes created by the lead smelting made the area unhealthy - people were probably dying from lead poisoning – and the settlement moved slowly west towards the site of the present town of Flint.

Above right: Medieval mill
Below right: Lead smelter

[1]*Henry Taylor Historic Notices, page 10*
[2]*Domesday Book*

Chapter 2

Edward I and Llywelyn ap Gruffydd

The 13th century Welsh prince, **Llywelyn ap Gruffydd**, a descendant of Roderic the Great, had a great influence on the area. He came from a noble pedigree, the son of Gruffydd ap Llywelyn and Senena, whose roots can be traced back to Cunedda and Coel the Old, who lived during the fifth century and whose ancestors date back to Roman times. Llywelyn was the second of four sons; Owain ap Gruffydd was the eldest and the two younger brothers were Dafydd ap Gruffydd and Rhodri ap Gruffydd.

The family was a divided one. Gruffydd was the eldest son of Llywelyn the Great but had been held hostage as a boy by King John of England and his father had made his second son, Dafydd ap Llywelyn, his successor instead. When Dafydd became Prince of Gwynedd, he also imprisoned his brother Grufydd, and when Henry III of England invaded the Welsh Borders, Gruffydd became his prisoner and was held in the Tower of London, along with his son Owain. Gruffydd died whilst trying to escape from the tower in 1244, which triggered Dafydd to rebel against Henry. Llywelyn fought alongside his uncle and when Dafydd ap Llywelyn died in 1246 without leaving an heir, Llywelyn was his natural successor, as his elder brother Owain, although now free, was not in Wales. The family divisions continued and there were many disputes between Llywelyn and his brothers throughout his reign.

Together, Llywelyn and Owain made terms with Henry, accepting restrictions on their territories that kept them to the west of the

Llywelyn the Great is reputed to have enjoyed stag hunting in Gwydyr Forest

Henry was not a strong king and, in 1263, his barons, led by Simon de Montfort, revolted against him with some success. The rebellion eventually failed and de Montfort was killed by Prince Edward at the Battle of Evesham in 1265. Llywelyn had formed an alliance with de Montfort, supplying Welsh troops and so was at risk of reprisal. While Henry was still recovering from the rebellion, Llywelyn continued his attacks eastwards, in order to strengthen his bargaining position. In 1267, he negotiated peace and was recognised by King Henry as Prince of Wales. (Later, on 13th October 1278, Llywelyn married Eleanor, the daughter of Simon de Montford, which did not help his already fraught relationship with Edward.)

In 1272, King Henry died and his son was crowned King Edward I on August 19th 1274, when he returned to England from a crusade.

Llywelyn's stormy relationship with Edward I, had a profound influence on the history of the area, changing its course completely. Their long-standing conflict brought about Edward's invasion of North Wales and the building of his formidable ring of seaward castles, of which Flint was the first.

Edward was a very different character from his father. When he became king, he was already a seasoned military leader and determined to have a stronger control of

Conwy. However, they soon broke with him in protest against the ruthless raids being conducted on the Welsh border.

When younger brother Dafydd came of age, the family disputes flared again. King Henry offered Dafydd lands within the already reduced Gwynedd but Llywelyn refused to accept this. Owain and Dafydd formed an alliance and rose against their brother but were defeated. Llywelyn continued to extend his territories east of the Conwy, recapturing most of north-east Wales, which had been given by Henry to his son, **Prince Edward**. This included the land that later became Flint.

Above left:
Artist's impression of
Llywelyn ap Gruffydd

Below: Knights returning
from crusade

Above: Edward I in battledress (copied from his seal)

Wales than his weaker father. This soon brought him into dispute with Llywelyn.

As a Welsh prince who considered himself an equal to Edward in terms of his lineage, Llywelyn did not feel the need to consult an English king on matters relating to Wales, whether it was the need to create a market, build a castle or manor house or even instigate new laws. This primary source clearly demonstrates his view,

> *And the aforesaid Prince Llywelyn declared that the fact that each province under the lord king's dominion – the Gascons in Gascony, the Scots in Scotland, the Irish in Ireland and the English in England – has its own laws and customs, according to the mode and usage of those parts in which they are situate, amplified rather than*

---

[3]*The Welsh Assize Rolls 1277-84, page 266*

diminished the Crown. In the same wise he seeks to have his own Welsh law and to be able to proceed by it, especially as the lord king had of his own free will in the peace made between them, granted their own law to him and to all Welshmen. As a matter of common right the Welsh, like these other nations subject to the king's governance, ought to have their own laws and customs according to their race.[3]

Llywelyn was summoned four times to pay homage to Edward I, firstly to Chester in August 1275, to Westminster in October 1275, to Winchester in January 1276 and finally to Westminster in April 1276, but he failed to turn up each time. (It was normal practice in those days to be summoned to pay homage as a demonstration of allegiance to the King.) In his defence, Llywelyn had attended a prior meeting arranged at Shrewsbury in November 1274, but Edward had not attended, due to illness. Had this meeting taken place the impending war between these two people of differing royal bloodlines might not have occurred and the story of Flint could have been very different. However, because of Llywelyn's presumed disrespect, the conflict escalated and Edward pursued his downfall. At the council at Westminster the decision was taken to make war on Llywelyn; a formal feudal summons was issued on the 12th December 1276. The king asked for all those who owed service to him to muster at Worcester by 1st July. Llywelyn's downfall was quite inevitable.

Edward invaded from Chester with a well-equipped and organised force of 15,000, marching along the North Wales coast and sending his fleet to surround Anglesey, from where Llywelyn got most of his grain. Llywelyn retreated into Snowdonia to raise an army but was forced to surrender when he was surrounded by Edward's army and cut off from his food supply. In the Treaty of Aberconwy in November 1277, he had to give up the lands he had conquered, withdrawing back into Gwynedd, west of the Conwy.

Llywelyn's younger brother, Dafydd, had fought with Edward against his brother but felt unfairly treated when English lords were given more power. In 1282, he changed sides and attacked nearby Hawarden Castle. This triggered a fierce rebellion across North Wales with Llywelyn and Dafydd fighting together against Edward's forces.

At first the Welsh armies made good progress moving eastwards towards Chester. The land around Flint would have been in the thick of the conflict. Llywelyn and his supporters attacked the partly constructed castle and sacked the town, burning many of the houses. Eventually however, Edward's immense army proved too strong for the rebels and Edward regained control.

Artist's impression of Dafydd ap Gruffydd

Dafydd was betrayed to Edward by his own men and, as punishment for his treachery, was the first man in Britain to be hung drawn and quartered. Llywelyn's fate was sealed on December 11th 1282 near the River Yrfon when he was killed by Stephen of Frankton, a Shropshire man who did not know the identity of the man he had killed.[4]

> *Sire, Know that the stout men whom you assigned to my command fought against Llywelyn ap Gruffudd in the region of Builth on Friday next after the feast of St. Nicholas and that Llywelyn ap Gruffudd is dead, his army vanquished and the whole flower of his army killed, as the bearer of this letter will tell you and have credence in what he will tell you on my part.*[5]

Edward's decision to build a series of castles across North Wales was an integral part of his plan to conquer and retain control of Wales. All Edwards's castles were strategically positioned one day's march apart starting with Flint, then Rhuddlan, Conwy, Beaumaris, Caernarfon and Harlech. Should any of his castles come under attack, reinforcements could also be supplied by sea, within a matter of days.

When his invasion began, the call went out for an enormous workforce to be assembled at the site of his first castle, the place that later became known as Flint. This opened up a new chapter in the history of our town.

[4]*Oxford History of England The Thirteenth Century, page 428*
[5]*Edward I and Wales. Welsh History and its Sources, page 60, Trevor Herbert & Gareth Elwyn Jones*

Wales in 1267

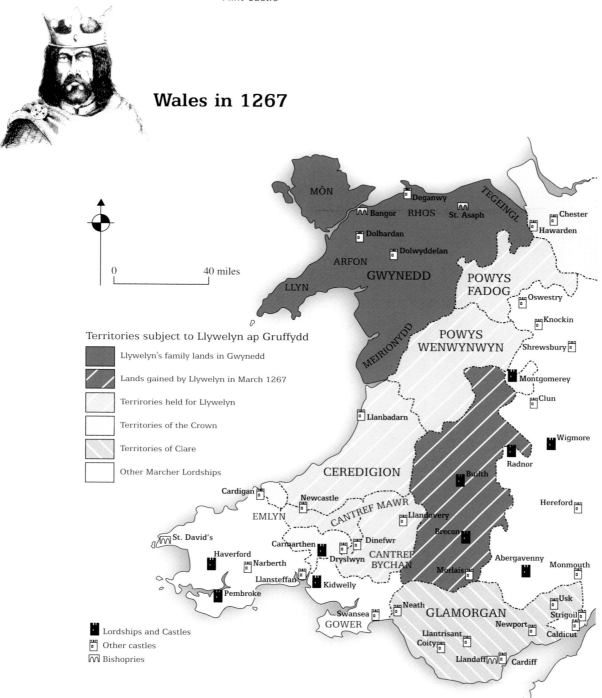

MÔN

Deganwy
Bangor RHOS St. Asaph TEGEINGL
Chester
Hawarden
Dolbardan
Dolwyddelan
ARFON
LLYN GWYNEDD POWYS FADOG
Oswestry
MEIRIONYDD Knockin
POWYS WENWYNWYN Shrewsbury
Montgomerey
Clun
Llanbadarn Wigmore
Radnor
CEREDIGION Builth
Hereford
Cardigan
Newcastle CANTREF MAWR Llandovery
EMLYN Dinefwr Brecon
St. David's Carmarthen CANTREF BYCHAN
Haverford Dryslwyn Morlais Abergavenny Monmouth
Narberth Neath Usk
Llansteffan Kidwelly GLAMORGAN Strigoil
Pembroke Newport Caldicut
Swansea Llantrisant
GOWER Coity
Llandaff Cardiff

0 ——————— 40 miles

Territories subject to Llywelyn ap Gruffydd

- Llywelyn's family lands in Gwynedd
- Lands gained by Llywelyn in March 1267
- Terrirories held for Llywelyn
- Territories of the Crown
- Territories of Clare
- Other Marcher Lordships

- ■ Lordships and Castles
- ▫ Other castles
- ᙡ Bishopries

These two maps show the land ownership in 1267 and 1277, show how much land Llywelyn had lost control of following his defeat by Edward I in 1277.

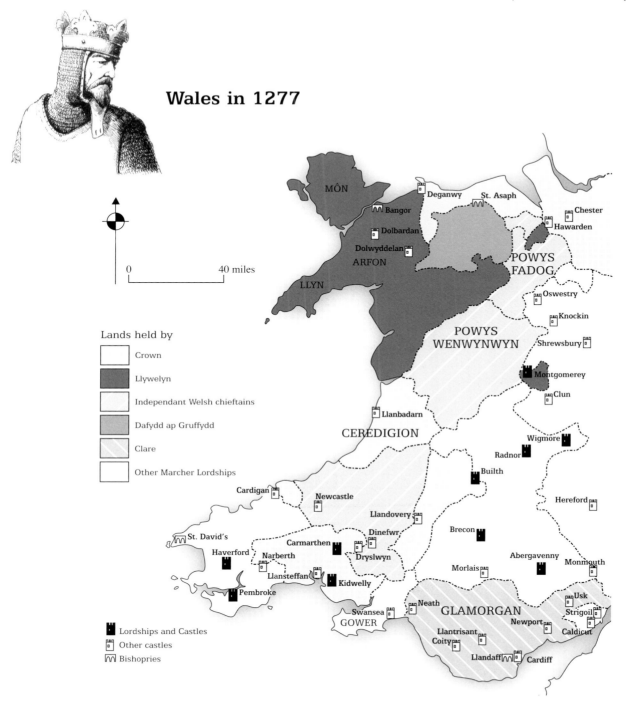

Wales in 1277

Lands held by

- Crown
- Llywelyn
- Independant Welsh chieftains
- Dafydd ap Gruffydd
- Clare
- Other Marcher Lordships

■ Lordships and Castles
□ Other castles
⋒ Bishopries

0   40 miles

MÔN

Deganwy   St. Asaph

Bangor

Chester

Dolbardan   Hawarden

Dolwyddelan

ARFON   POWYS FADOG

LLYN

Oswestry

Knockin

POWYS WENWYNWYN

Shrewsbury

Montgomerey

Clun

Llanbadarn

CEREDIGION

Wigmore

Radnor

Builth

Cardigan

Newcastle

Hereford

Llandovery

St. David's

Dinefwr

Brecon

Carmarthen

Haverford   Narberth

Abergavenny   Monmouth

Dryslwyn

Morlais

Llansteffan

Kidwelly

Usk

Pembroke

Neath   GLAMORGAN

Strigoil

Swansea

Newport   Caldicut

GOWER

Llantrisant

Coity

Llandaff   Cardiff

Chapter 3

The Building of Flint Castle

Once Edward made his decision to build a castle at Flint, he quickly gathered the necessary workforce from across England. It was hostile territory and a substantial force was required to guard the site and control the workforce. The Cinque Ports fleet, consisting of twenty-six ships, were the first to arrive in Chester, followed by 800 cavalry and 2500 infantrymen. Edward himself arrived in Chester on 15th July, 1277.

Knights had been sent out in advance with orders to impress specific craftsmen who were required for this mammoth task, as many did not come willingly. If they did not agree to join Edward's workforce, their homes were burnt to the ground leaving them with little option but to join the growing army of craftsmen or stay and starve. The impressed workers were moved swiftly northwards to join the awaiting troops at Chester, a veritable army of woodcutters, diggers, dykers and masons, gathered from Leicester, Lincoln, Nottingham, Warwick, Salop, Stafford, Lancaster, Chester and Devizes.

We are fortunate that a detailed picture of the workforce employed in the Welsh castle building can be built up as so many of the original payrolls still exist. They are an invaluable primary source of information when trying to trace the workers and skills that were required in the building of these complicated fortresses. It is possible not only to glean information about the pay of individual workers but also their names, the dates they were paid and the castle they were working at. The records also show that, in some cases, they moved from castle to castle as Edward's ambitious building programme progressed.

William Perton, who had recruited mason's for the building programme, became the King's Clerk after the initial build at Flint and can be traced on many of the payrolls.

Edward I's decision to build his first castle at Flint on the banks of the River Dee, and his subsequent founding the town alongside it, helped the area to grow and prosper.

WORKFORCE	General Information	Recruited	Where
Master William of Perton	Was given expenses and set out from High Wycombe	MASONS	Leicester, Lincoln Nottingham
Master Robert of Belvoir	Sent to 'Divers' parts of the Realm	CARPENTERS	Warwick, Leicester, Salop, Stafford, Lancaster, Cheshire
Third Clerk	Referred to as M.Clericus	DIGGERS	Cheshire
John of Sponfford		WOODMEN	

Why did he choose this particular site for his first foothold in North Wales, I hear you ask? It was one day's march from the main garrison at Chester, approximately ten miles across the flat marshland. Supplies could be brought in by boat along the River Dee and this was vital as the surrounding land was hostile territory.

The castle is built on a natural plinth of rock, which originally jutted out into the River Dee. Not only was there a natural ford in the river at this point to cross to his small fort and garrison at Ness, but there was also a quarry at Ness, which could supply most of the sandstone used for the magnificent stonework. Another advantage of the chosen site was that the land did not belong to the Welsh Princes but was held by Earl Hugh, an ancestor of the present Duke of Westminster.

The area that surrounded the site of the proposed castle was abundant with the natural resources required for the enormous construction task. Lead ore was mined locally and had been smelted near the proposed site of the castle and at Pentre-Ffwrn-Dan, Oakenholt, since Roman times. Lime for mortar was plentiful to the west, just a stone's throw from the proposed site, and some sandstone was available on the site with plenty more at Ness Quarry.

Right: Bringing the stone across the Dee from Ness Quarry (Chris Hull)

Some of the workforce who were assembled at Chester made their way via Shotwick Ford where there was a natural crossing of the riverbed, crossing the salt marsh flats at low tide. The Cheshire woodcutters came along the shore, cutting out a roadway through the dense scrub that lined the riverside at that time. This roadway could then be used to bring supplies overland.

Other woodcutters were dispatched to the Forest of Toxteth to start felling the trees needed to build the stockade to enclose the proposed new town. Wood was also needed to construct the lifting engines that were used to place the large sandstone blocks (very different from the modern lifting equipment that we have today).

A large army was required to implement the castle-building project; a large fleet of ships to supply all the things needed and a contingent of knights and infantrymen to police the assembled workforce. The sheer numbers deployed were enough to have frightened any Welshman thinking of protesting at King Edward's arrival onto Welsh soil. The few fishermen, who lived and worked their nets on the shores of the River Dee were easily persuaded to leave their small hovels and move further inland.

The conditions that the impressed workforce lived in must have been quite appalling. No modern sanitation for them; they would have slept, worked and eaten on site, and been guarded twenty-four hours per day, as I am sure many of them would have wished to abscond. Their days would have been long and they would have worked from dawn to past dusk to fulfil Edwards's ambitions to create his ring of iron around Wales. I am sure many of the workforce would have lived in constant fear, both from the masters who ruled them and from the locals who, I am sure, would also have wished them harm.

By 25th July 1277, camp was set up on the foreshore near the proposed site. Edward moved his base to Basingwerk near the abbey, where he stayed for a few months observing the initial stages of the build.

The first written reference to Flint was in Latin *Nostrum castellum supra fluent* (our castle above the tide). It later became known as Flint or, in Welsh, Y Fflint. Flint rock is easily split and the name may be a reference to the area as Edward's first slice of Wales.

The architect or master mason was Richard L'Engenour (Richard of Chester) who was a leading military engineer of his time who worked on many of Edward I's projects. He is credited with working on Chester Cathedral in 1310[6], the weirs at Chester and royal works throughout Cheshire. Edward held him in high esteem, granting him the Dee Mills in 1275, accompanied with the provision to grind corn free of toll in time of war. He farmed the Dee Mills and fisheries until his death in 1315.

Richard was the founder of the Belgrave family and an ancestor of the Duke of Westminster.[7] He was made Mayor of Chester in 1304. He had three sons Nicholas, Egidius and Giles, and a daughter named after his wife, Agnes. They lived at Parr Hall, a mansion next to St. Olaves Church in Lower Bridge Street, but he also held property in Bridge Street and Watergate Street, and owned three farms; 50 acres of land in Hoole, and also land in Eccleston and Pulford.

Most historians credit Master James of St George with the design of all the castles built in Wales by Edward I. However, in the case of Flint, this is a false claim as Master James of St George did not arrive in England until the spring of 1278, when a full building season had already taken place at Flint.[8,9] The payrolls provide evidence of this. Special payments were made to the workers, between August 2nd and the 10th 1277, to men who "bestirred themselves" carrying handbarrows. Further payments were made on August 10th 1277, for their advanced work rate for setting out the foundations of the towers and raising timber to form a palisade on the high recommendation of Otho de Grandison, a friend and councillor to Edward, on the orders of the king.[10]

It is documented that Master James did not enter the payroll of Flint Castle until November 1st 1280. On contrast, the payrolls show that Richard L'Engenour was paid from day one of the build at a rate of one shilling per day, which suggests that he had overall control of the first stages of the build.

---

[6]*Chester Cathedral – History Archives, page 7 www.chestercathedral./ freeserve.co.uk/history*

[7]*Later Medieval Chester 1230 –1550, City and Crown*

[8]*The Castles of St George Esperache, AJ Taylor, Antiquaries Jur.XXXiii 1953, for dates on Master James's arrival in England.*

[9]*History of the King's Works, page 204*

[10]*Vincencio clerico pro duobus solidis quos dedit diversis hominibus precepto O.de Grandson marerolo leuando apud Flind.ijs'*

Otho de Grandison 1218 –1328

Otho was the son of Peter, Lord of Grandison near Lausanne, and became a very important person in the life of Edward I. He entered Edward's service on the death of his own father when he was no more than twenty years old. He appears as one of Edward's own knights in 1268[11], fighting under Edward at Lewes and Evesham and also accompanying him on the Crusades at Acre in 1271. When Edward survived an assassination attempt on June 18th 1272, Otho was the one who sucked the poison from the wounded Edward and was rewarded by being named as one of Edwards's executors.

At the start of the campaign against Llywelyn, he served as a banneret (someone who occupies the middle ground between a Baron and a Knight) under the Earl of Lincoln[12], with four knights and ten troopers as his personal followers plus a number of lances. He was put in charge of operations on Anglesey. This was a major posting as it stifled the food chain to Llywelyn and his men as, at that time, Anglesey was the breadbasket of North Wales. It was also important because it had command of the sea, enabling Edward to advance to Bangor and Caernarfon and Harlech. When peace was declared, Otho was made Justiciar of North Wales.

At the start of the building of Flint Castle in 1277, Otho was granted the Channel Islands as a lordship for life along with lands in England and Ireland. Otho was the instigator of the building of the

[11]*Calendar of Charter Rolls ii.140.177*

[12]*Sir Otho de Grandson, Royal Historical Society, page 131*

town walls near St Mary's Church, Co. Tipperary, Ireland where he held land at Okonagh. He also owned the town of Tipperary and castle and land of Kilfekle, in 1298 whilst he was Lord of the Manor. He also owned a house at Westminster with tenements in London and lands in Kent and was Mayor of Caernarfon in 1291-2.

He lived until he was over 90 years old and is buried at St Mary's, Ottery. From his long association with Edward he became very rich and powerful and was well respected amongst his contemporaries.

A prophecy was told at his birth by a person described as 'one full of superstition or divine inspiration'. They took a brand or twig from the fire and said, 'as long as this brand lasts the baby shall live', and the brand was set into the wall. It is told that when Otho reached the great age of ninety he said he did not want to live any longer and the brand was taken from the wall and thrown onto the fire. No sooner the brand was consumed in the fire than Otho died.

He left provisions in his will for his wife Beatrice and his children. Thomas was left 4 oxen and 200 sheep, William was left 10 marcs, and his daughter was left six dishes, 6 saucers and 4 silver cups. Otho left a strange request in his will that on the day of his burial he wished for no armed men or horse to go before his body and for his corpse to only be covered with a white cloth marked with a red cross for he was a member of the order of the Knights Templar.

A Templar knight - the shield bears the coat of arms of Otto de Grandison

PERSON IN CHARGE	TITLE	TRADE	NUMBER	PAY PER DAY
Peter de Brompton	Twenty Men	Dyker	16	4d
Peter de Brompton	Master	Dyker	4	6d
Peter de Brompton		Dyker	913	3d
Peter de Brompton		Smiths	4	4d
Peter de Brompton		Smiths Boys	8	2d
Hugh de Creton	Twenty Men	Carpenter working in the forest of Toxteth	35	4d
Hugh de Creton		Carpenter working in the forest of Toxteth	100	3d
Walter de Jaye	Twenty Men	Carpenters with the Army Carpenters	11	4d
Robert de Belvero		Mason	230	3d
Thomas de Graham	Master	Masons	1	6d
Thomas de Graham		Woodcutters	200	4d
Gilbert de Brideshale	Twenty Men	Woodcutters	16	4d
Gilbert de Brideshale		Woodcutters	320	3d

Workforce week one, 25th July, 1277

The workforces were placed under the control of various knights, and split into groups under their twenty men (foremen). These two tables (above and overleaf), made up from information on the King's Payrolls, show the workforce in week one and two of the building works.

Peter de Brompton seemed to have the major part of the responsibility for the men, having the most men to pay and supervise.

In week one of the build a total of 1858 men were involved in the first stage of the building of the castle. Most were dykers who were required to help prevent the water from filling in the newly dug foundations. The first order of 10,000 sandstone blocks was placed at the quarry of Ness prior to 25th July 1277. Large numbers of carpenters and wood cutters were employed, some working in the forests at Toxteth cutting the timber and building the 250 rafts needed to transport the stone across the river. Many others were working on site, constructing the stockade required to keep the men safe and making the lifting machinery to move the sandstone blocks into place. There were also numerous masons, working the stones delivered from Ness Quarry. Smiths were employed to make and mend the metal tools required for the project.

The Workforce

By week two, the workforce had increased dramatically to 2,911, indicating the urgency of making the site safe. More specialist workers were brought to the site, such as Carbonarii (miners) to mine the coal to fuel the smith's fires. The number of dykers working on the site doubled, including a group from Holland. The two assistant Dutch dykers were paid an incredible 8d each, nearly three times as much as the other dykers. One can only wonder what dangerous or specialised task they were involved in!

PERSON IN CHARGE	TITLE	TRADE	NUMBER	PAY PER DAY
Peter de Brompton	Master	Dyker	2	6d
Peter de Brompton	Assistant	Dyker	1	5d
Peter de Brompton		Dyker	1520	3d
Peter de Brompton	Twenty Men	Dyker	7	4d
Peter de Brompton		Smiths	4	4d
Peter de Brompton		Smiths Boys	8	2d
Peter de Brompton		Constable	1	6d
Peter de Brompton		Constables Men	100	4d
Peter de Brompton	Master	Carbonarii	1	5d
Peter de Brompton		Carbonarii (miners)	5	4d
Peter de Brompton		Cinder Carriers working at speed	2	3d
Robert de Belvero	Twenty Men	Carpenters	11	4d
Robert de Belvero		Carpenters	230	3d
Robert de Belvero		Wood-cutters	100	3d
Thomas de Graham	Master	Mason	1	6d
Thomas de Graham		Masons	200	4d
Gilbert de Brideshale	Twenty Men	Wood-cutters	16	4d
Gilbert de Brideshale		Wood-cutters	400	3d
W.de Sancto Botulpho		Dyker (from Hoylande)	300	3d
W.de Sancto Botulpho	Assistant	Dyker	2	8d

Workforce week two, 1st August, 1277

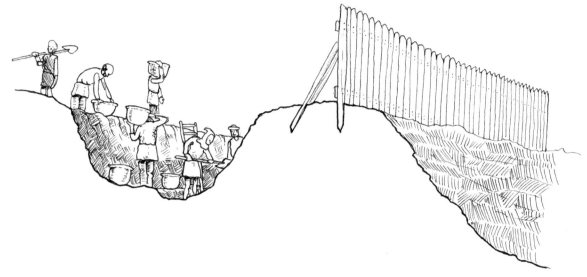

Cinder carriers were paid for working at speed, which suggests the urgency for the foundations to be in place must have increased.

A constable with one hundred men was brought in, presumably to ensure the tools and workforce did not abscond, for this was a frequent occurrence with workforces who were impressed into Edward's army of workers.

By 1280, more workers were impressed into Edward's army of craftsmen as his building programme grew at apace, brought from Cumberland, Derby, Essex, Gloucester, Northumberland, Oxford, Rutland, Warwick, Wiltshire and Yorkshire. All gathered at the staging point of Chester. Some were brought to Flint, others continued to his other castles now under construction.

Many specialists were brought in as the work progressed. Some examples are given below:

John le Blund (White) of London was paid 19 shillings for dressing 152 serchers (concave stones) for the well in the Great Tower.

Peter Morel was paid 12 shillings for dressing stones for the heads of three windows in the South West Tower.

Ingeram dressed stones called roydes for 13 ½ feet of the South West Tower.

Flauner and Thomas de Hardingesham dressed stones for the doorways and steps of the Great Tower at 1 ¼ d per stone.

John Page, John of Clifford and Richard of Wellingborough were paid 6s 3d for making eight embrasures (openings) with arrow slits in the curtain walls, and one at 7s 3d (which I assume was the larger barrel-vaulted embrasure alongside the North West Tower, described on page 34).

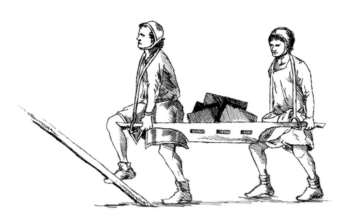

Master Henry of Oxford, a master carpenter, carted wood, which was made into brattices[13] (a covered gallery fixed to the top of a tower, used for defence).

It took until 1282 before the castle was near to completion. The pay rolls indicate that the Donjon Tower required a temporary roof consisting of 44 bundles of straw thatch, bought by Master Henry of Alcester, and spars were purchased to hold the thatch down.

The whole castle was limewashed making it appear white and shimmering, which added to its awesome appearance. Fragments of the limewash can still be seen in parts of the castle that have been protected from weathering such as in the basement of the Donjon Tower.

In the summer of 1284, the construction of the Kings Chamber in the Great Tower was well under way making ready for his visit in the September of that year. The roof received a covering of lead by the plumbers between 8th September and the 30th November 1286 which completed the work on the tower. Fifteen cart loads of lead for the roofing of this tower was bought from Sutton of Flint, who also carried stone from the fields for the defence of the castle.

[13]*Flintshire Historical Society Publication (1957), pages 37-8*

Two hundred planks and three hundred boards were made into parapets upon the walls towards the sea. Repairs were made to the outer bridge which was thirty feet in length, and a new bridge was built between the Donjon Tower and inner bailey. A great wheel for drawing water from the well and a new door for the Eagle Tower was also made. They also completed hanging the windows in the battlements in the inner bailey.

The defences around the town were improved during the same period as the castle and town were still at risk of attack from the Welsh forces. The town stockade was repaired, another stockade was added on the Chester side and steps made upon the walls near the sea.

The payrolls show that between 23rd August 1277 and 25th December 1286 £6068 7s 5¾ d was paid with a further payment added of £722 13s 5d from the 25th July to 1277[14]. This brought the total cost of the castle building to: £6791 0s 5¾d, which was an enormous amount of money in those days (around 4.5 million pounds in today's terms).

Further improvements and maintenance continued. Mason, Geoffrey de Boneville, made a wall between the Donjon Tower and inner bailey in 1302–3. He was paid 5 shillings per hundred stones, except for 320

stones where he was paid 4s 6d. I assume that the cheaper batch were either smaller stones or needed less dressing.

In 1325 carpenter, Master Richard de Legh, worked on the repairs at Flint Castle together with plasterer, Master John de Helpeston.

A careful examination of the castle ruins shows how the walls were constructed and reveals the range of materials used. The thick castle walls consisted of an outer and inner face of dressed sandstone blocks, infilled with rubble. This central core of rubble contained numerous other rocks, including beach pebbles, old tiles, broken pieces of sandstone and rubble from other buildings.

Mostly the sandstone is golden sandstone and often contains nodules of iron, but there are also slabs of red Cheshire Sandstone.

---

[14]*A Postscript Flintshire Historical Publication (1958), pages 38-40, A.J. Taylor*

Chapter 4

A Visual Tour of the Castle

This visual tour has been included to help you appreciate the unique qualities of Flint Castle and to understand the interesting features that still remain.

From the castle entrance the tour is described in a clockwise direction, but you may wish to follow your own path.

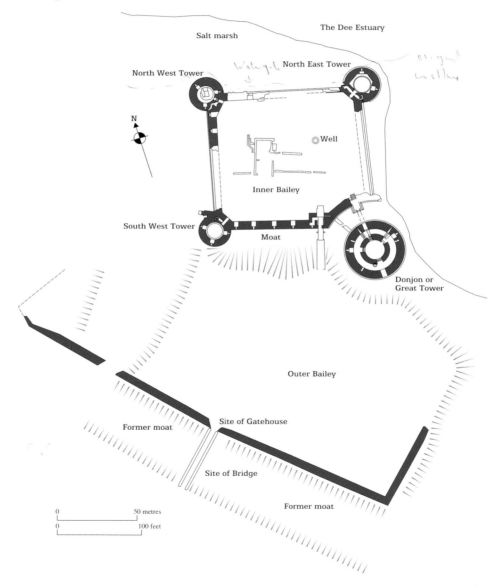

Plan of the remains today

North West Tower

North East Tower

South West Tower

The Donjon or Great Tower

Aerial view of the castle remains, 1987

Glossary of terms

inner bailey – the flat area enclosed within the castle walls (now grassed)

outer bailey – the flat area between the inner castle walls and the outer gatehouse and moat (now grassed)

barrel vaulted – a semi-circular roof

battlements – a wall built between the towers that soldiers could walk along

curtain wall – the outer wall of the main castle, connecting the towers

embrasure – an opening with an arrowslit in it where soldiers on duty would sit and keep an eye on what was happening outside the castle

garderobe – a medieval toilet, a kind of cupboard, usually with a stone seat, with a chute that discharged into a cesspit or the moat, depending on the structure of the building

watergate – an opening in the outer wall with stairs leading down to the water's edge

moat – a deep water-filled ditch (now dry) that surrounded the castle

piscina – hand basin for washing communion vessels, usually set against or into a wall, beside an altar

The outer gatehouse and outer bailey

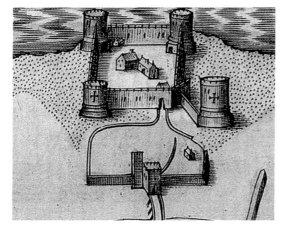

Above: View of the castle from John Speed's map, 1621, showing the tall gatehouse and battlements all around the outer bailey (courtesy of the National Library of Wales)

From Castle Dyke Street (the road in front of the castle) follow the clear path leading towards the castle. This takes you through the site of the outer gatehouse and across the outer bailey to the castle entrance.

The sea gave good natural protection from the north but the southerly side was more vulnerable. To give it additional protection an outer wall with a tall stone gatehouse and moat was constructed. This outer gatehouse was strategic to the security of the castle and its occupants. Its importance was confirmed in June 1281 with the appointment of its custody being awarded to Ralf of Broughton.[15] Little now remains as it was blown up by the Parliamentarian forces after the Civil War, around 1646, to prevent it being re-garrisoned.

The outer bailey would have housed a large hall for the troops stationed at the castle with a brew house, kitchen and bakery. The horses would also have been housed here.

Flint Castle is unique because it has two moats, the inner moat protecting the main castle and the outer moat protecting the entrance from the town. Both moats would have been much wider and filled with sea water at high tide.

Above: The entrance to the castle may have looked similar to this one at Aigues Mortes in France (compare with the John Speed's drawing above it).

[15]*Cal. Welsh Rolls p 189*

The inner gatehouse and inner bailey

Having crossed the outer bailey, you now enter the main castle via a modern timber bridge that has replaced the drawbridge that would originally have crossed the inner moat.

Notice a recess in the castle walls to the left of the main entrance. This is the location of the inner gatehouse. This area was crucial to the security of the castle, protecting the interior from attack. The inner gatehouse was used as a lookout point to see who was arriving at the drawbridge, 'friend or foe'. It would have been constantly manned and the guards would have only raised the portcullis when they had checked that the visitors were friendly. During the day the drawbridge would usually have been lowered but could quickly be raised if the castle was under attack.

Nothing remains of the portcullis or drawbridge but, if you study the stonework on the right of the entrance you can see the rebating for the mechanism that raised the drawbridge and a long vertical groove indicates the postition of the portcullis.

The inner bailey is a rectangular enclosure that would have housed a hall, chapel, kitchen, bakehouse and brewhouse, which would have been built against the curtain walls. Battlements originally went all around the inner bailey and are still clearly visible although far lower nowadays.

The stone foundations in the inner bailey are from later buildings when the castle was used as a small factory.

Below: The castle entrance

Right: Remains of the well in the inner bailey

Far right: Remains of the well in the basement of the Donjon Tower

The castle has two wells that were once supplied by fresh water from the Swinchard Brook. The main well is situated in the inner bailey, and the other is inside the Donjon Tower. I have measured the depth of them and they go down over 20 feet, and I am sure they were originally much deeper. The separate Donjon Tower well ensured that those living in that tower did not have to mix with the rest of the inhabitants of the castle.

South West Tower - The Prison or Little Tower

The South West Tower is sometimes recorded in the payroll for the castle as the Little Tower or the Prison Tower so one must assume that is where prisoners were kept before a gaol was built on the outer bailey. This tower was built in a different manner to the other towers. The rebating on the outside of the tower indicates that a doorway once existed and was closed from the inner bailey side, thus locking the prisoners inside.

As you walk into the tower you are looking down into the basement area where prisoners were probably held. The basement did not have any steps, which suggests that the poor prisoners may have been thrown down there and left to rot!

The tower originally extended to the outer bailey walls and prisoners may have been taken straight out of the castle and away through the woods to where the gallows were situated.

There would have originally been three floors. The top floor would have led to the battlements that originally went all around the inner bailey. There is evidence of a spiral staircase, which led to the upper floor and the battlements.

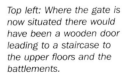

Top left: Where the gate is now situated there would have been a wooden door leading to a staircase to the upper floors and the battlements.

Bottom left: This is the South West curtain wall taken from the inner bailey with the remains of two embrasures, which incorporated arrowslits. To the right you can make out the holes that would have held the rebating for the outer doorway of the South West Tower.

Bottom far left: Detail of an arrowslit. You can see where it has been widened to fit a crossbow. Looking at the arrowslits gives a good idea of the line of vision of the bowman. It would have been easy to fire out but very difficult to fire into them.

All these marks can be seen in the first embrasure near the South West Tower

Right: B. Davies 1858

Middle right: H Owen 1858

Bottom right: E Lewis 1845

One embrasure in the southern curtain wall, next to the Prison Tower, is covered in graffiti from different periods, including some that are over 150 years old. Whilst I would be concerned if any more modern graffiti, made with pens and spray paint, is added, these early names are intriguing and add to the castle's story. Some have been very carefully cut into the stone, some showing some skill with carving and lettering.

We cannot be certain why this particular embrasure has so much graffiti. It is certainly fairly sheltered so the graffiti has not been worn away and offers good views to the town, ensuring that you didn't get caught in the act. Perhaps some was done by young lads, hoping to leave a reminder of their time spent down the castle, then others just followed their trend?

The story behind one signature has been uncovered. Early in the nineteenth century an old gentleman, who was a retired minister from America, came to visit Flint and addressed one of the weeknight services. He told the audience that he had been born in Flint and had seen the first train ever to go through Flint. He also told them that as a boy he used to play in the castle, and that he had cut his name on a stone there. It can be found in an alcove on the west side: *Edward Lewis 1845*

The North West or Garrison Tower

The North West Tower housed the garrison, hence its alternative name. This tower was strategic for the safety of the castle and those who lived and worked inside. The tower contained lots of offset embrasures, giving 180° vision, so it would have been a good position from which to defend the castle if attacked from the sea. In 1277 it was occupied by the Chester archers who were renowned for their fighting skills.

It had good access, compared to the other towers so that soldiers could quickly move into position, or collect weapons, as needed.

There are four point of entry into this tower.

1. From the steps in the Inner Bailey, down into the basement

2. From the watergate that once existed to the right, giving good access from the sea

3. From the spiral staircase to the left

4. From the larger embrasure next to the tower in the inner bailey

The weapons were probably stored in the basement and the steps from the inner bailey would have given swift access to them. A ring of stonework along the inside base of the tower may have been used to stack bows and crossbows to raise them off the floor and stop them getting wet when supplies delivered by sea were being brought in.

Above: The South West Tower from the inner bailey

Right: Steps down to the basement from the inner bailey

Far right: Stone ledge on the basement floor

Top left: View from the North West Tower, showing the small windows that looked onto the inner bailey

Top middle left: The barrel-vaulted embrasure beside the North West Tower is bigger than the others, allowing two or three soldiers at a time to run through to the tower to collect their weapons if the castle was attacked. Some of the smaller embrasures have arched roofs, which were a later design.

Top left: A well-preserved embrasure at Aigues Mortes. The seats on either side gave the soldiers a chance to rest when it was quiet.

Left: The location of the remains of the watergate in the northern wall.

Below: Looking along the remains of the northern wall, where the watergate was situated. It is hard to imagine when the sea washed against these walls and boats were unloaded here!

Looking inside the tower, see if you can see the two large holes above the embrasure once held the floor joists that supported the upper floor of this tower.

You can also clearly see the remains of the hooded fireplace that once existed on the upper floor of the tower.

The two small windows above the tower entrance were lookout windows onto the inner bailey to ensure the workers were working and check that the area was safe.

The Watergate

Above: Artist's impression of the castle from the sea, showing the watergate.

Moving clockwise from the Garrison Tower, you can see the site of the original watergate that existed until around 1304 when the sea started to recede from the castle at low tide. It would have been a vital part of the castle because most of the supplies needed for the running of the castle would have been delivered here by boat. It would have originally had a set of steps leading to the outside of the North West Tower and from inside that tower, a platform would have protruded outside the castle walls down to the watergate for loading and unloading. You can still see the remains of the original steps which led down to where the boats would have docked. There was a second smaller watergate at the Donjon Tower.

The North East Tower or Eagle Tower

This view shows the North East Tower and also part of the natural plinth of rock that the castle stands on (Marsh Level). You can see that the battlements were originally much higher, reaching up to the to the first floor window of the tower (the middle window that you can see). Internally you can see that the tower was an irregular hexagon, unlike the more circular shape of the other towers.

It is interesting that the castle is in a ruined state, as it gives you the opportunity to see how it was constructed. If you look at the remains of the battlement walls you can see that the masons lined the outside of the walls with facing stones and filled the middle with rubble, including pebbles from the beach that would originally have been below the castle, before the river silted up and the saltmarsh developed.

The North East Tower was probably used as a guest tower because in its construction there are no arrow slits on the upper floors, just windows. It was three storeys in height with a basement that could only been entered by means of a trapdoor in the floor. You can see the remains of the spiral staircase would have led to the upper two floors and to the battlements.

The top floor was used as a bedroom with battlements above. The main living quarters were on the second floor, shaped like an irregular hexagon, and you can still see the

Above: The North East Tower

Right: The remains of the hooded fireplace

Far right: A hooded fireplace in Tour de Constance in France

blackened bricks in the hooded fireplace, evidence of fires that were once lit there.

The lower room would have been occupied by the servants, who would have attended the needs of the guests staying on the upper floors. Supplies used in the tower would have been kept in the basement where they would have remained dry. The well in the inner bailey was near at hand for visitors occupying this tower.

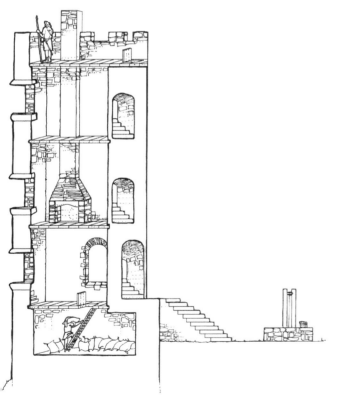

Above left: North East Tower showing a window and the holes for the ceiling supports in the wall below it

Above right: Looking up the former spiral staircase

Far left: Cross-section of the tower

Left: The North East Tower from the inner bailey taken from the same angle as the cross-section drawing

The Donjon or Great Tower

Above: The Donjon Tower

Right: Wall on the inner bailey side of the drawbridge that led to the Donjon Tower. The groove in the masonry held the roof of a wooden building.

Below right: This row of stone work between the Donjon Tower and the inner curtain wall is the base of a wall that kept the water level at a constant height so that boats could always be loaded and unloaded at the watergate.

The Donjon or Great Tower is unique in design, the only example of its kind in the country. It is offset and separate from the rest of the castle and could be isolated from it by raising its drawbridge. It was the last point of defence for the castle, a place of safety for its most important residents. It warrants a mention in the Guinness Book of Records for having the thickest walls of any castle, over 23 feet or 7metres thick in parts! (Measurements were taken from the entrance of the Donjon Tower through to the basement area.) Only the basement and part of an upper floor remain but it was once several stories high and may have had a smaller narrow tower on the top (see Aigues Mortes page 46).

The Donjon Tower was used as the residence for the Constable of the Castle, who later also became Mayor of Flint. Several royal visitors also stayed here; Edward I, his son Edward II, and Richard II. The tower had its own well and chapel and the upper floors where the Constable and special guests stayed afforded some comfort and privacy but were also secure and well guarded.

There is evidence of a small wooden building on the inner bailey side of the Donjon Tower drawbridge. It would have acted as a look out point onto the drawbridge and also as a station point for guards protecting the tower. Being made of wood, it could be set alight if the inner bailey of the castle came under

siege, giving an extra line of defence for the Donjon Tower.

When the estuary began to silt up and the sea receded from the castle, the main watergate on the northern wall of the castle was blocked off and the watergate in the Donjon Tower was used for off-loading supplies.

The basement of the Donjon Tower had a tall barrel-vaulted ceiling (over 12' high). It was lime washed to aid the limited natural light from the arrow slits and tallow torches would also have been used. You can still see the black marks made by the torches.

Stone steps lead from the central area up to three arched openings, that once led into tall wedge-shaped rooms. They would have been used for storage, possibly holding the supplies for the other castles that Edward was constructing.

The area below the modern metal steps would have been used to house livestock to be used for meat if the castle came under attack. Look for an upward facing shaft in the wall that was used to catch water to keep the animals watered. Cattle hide would have been placed on the other side to catch water which would have flowed into the area below the stairway. It would also have provided much needed air to this otherwise claustrophobic area.

Right: View of the basement showing the lower area beneath the metal steps on the left where livestock would have been kept.

Soldiers would have been responsible for feeding livestock and loading or off-loading ships docking at the watergate.

The circular central area of the basement would have been used for repairing the arrows used at the castle. In 1304, the records show that Richard the Attilator came from Chester to Flint Castle and repaired 10,000 arrows.

This tower has several well-preserved garderobes, medieval toilets. They would have discharged into the moat which was washed out at every tide (a forerunner of flush toilets?). The first you see as you approach the stairs that lead to the upper floor is separate from the others. I assume this was used by the soldiers and other staff who waited on those in residence. It is plainer in appearance than the more elaborate ones in the upper floor apartment, indicating that even as far back as 1277 there was a culture of 'them and us'!

The upper floor ones in the apartment had the luxury of having a door - one wonders about the ones used by the less privileged in the tower and also in the castle as a whole.

The garderobes would have had a stone or wooden bench seat with a central hole that discharged down a stone chute to the basement and out into the moat. If you look up the chute from the basement, you will see how they connect with the upper floors. It is from the era of the garderobe that you get the saying "look out below" for obvious reasons!

Below: The basement showing the central circular area and entrances to the tall storage area

Above: Illustration of a garderobe

Above left: Stairway to upper floor. The garderobe for soldiers on duty above the apartment is on the left and the chapel was located at the top of the stairs on the right.

Below far left: This is where there would have been a door to the upper apartment in the Donjon Tower, to keep it private from those working in the basement area and giving extra protection if the castle was attacked.

Below left: A garderobe in the royal appartment

Above: View across the Dee Marshes from the chapel area. The remains of the barrel-vaulted ceiling of the chapel can clearly be seen on the right.

The upper floor, whilst furnished in a much grander style, followed the same basic design pattern as the lower floors, having a central circular living area with smaller segment shaped rooms leading off. It was a private appartment equipped for the most important guests. It had three bedchambers, two garderobes, a kitchen area, a living area and a small chapel that looked across the Dee Marshes. It was here that Richard II heard mass on that fateful day when he was deposed and from where he saw Henry Bolingbroke and his supporters coming across the marshes to take him captive.

The central room was originally thatched but a cone shaped lead roof was added in 1286. The roof cover restricted light to this room and light would have been borrowed from the other rooms that surrounded it.

Top left: The remains of the piscina in the chapel wall can still be seen.

Top right: Looking into the chapel at Tour de Constance

Right: The upper floor appartment. Note the well-preserved garderobe. In the centre, below the garderobe, you can see the stone work that was the hearth of the grate that once existed in the central room in the middle of the upper floor.

Above: Tour de Constance in France

The massive tower of Tour de Constance at Aigues Mortes in Provence, France, is thought to have been the model for the Donjon Tower in Flint. When studying Flint Castle you have to consider where Edward I may have got his design ideas and it is likely to have been from Aigues Mortes. He spent three months there in 1270 awaiting the arrival of the fleet, which was to take him on a crusade.

Aigues Mortes is a walled town with a large offset tower, The Tour de Constance, which was originally used as a look out point. The tower was originally constructed with a drawbridge which helped to separate it from the town. Aigues Mortes' construction began in 1241, built as a staging point for the crusades. Later in its history it became famous for the incarceration of some of its prisoners. In October 13th 1685 the cells were occupied by 45 Templars and later in 1730 Marie Durand, the protestant protester, spent an incredible 38 years locked inside the tower![16]

The similarity between the Tour de Constance tower and the Donjon Tower at Flint Castle is quite remarkable; the French tower is offset from the town walls and the Donjon is offset from the rest of Flint Castle; both had some independence and could be separated by a drawbridge from the rest of the structure; both have two floors with inter communicating segment shaped rooms leading from a central area.

In 1985, as a primary source to verify this theory of similarity between the two towers, Alain Albaric, a renowned historian from Aigues-Mortes, came to Flint to study the Donjon Tower. He made precise measurements of the tower which were taken to a French university for analysis. When Alain contacted me with the results, I was amazed to find that Flint's tower was the exact same dimension as its sister tower at Aigues-Mortes.

It seems probable that, during the three months Edward spent in Aigues Mortes, he took the opportunity to study the Constance tower, and brought the design back to use in the construction of Flint's Donjon Tower. I believe he also brought some of the masons who worked on the Tour de Constance back with him so they could work on Flint Castle. Some of the masons' marks taken from the walls at Aigues Mortes are the same as ones found on the walls of Flint Castle.

Right: Mason's mark, Tour de Constance

Far right: Etching of Tour de Constance, from Inventaire General Des Monuments et Des Richesses Artiques De La France Aigues Mortes

[16]*Aigues-Mortes Tourist Guide 83 Chemin de L'Olivet Alain Abaric, Aigues-Mortes*

Masons' marks

The masons working on the castle carved marks into the stones. The marks identified the work of each mason so that the quality of their workmanship could be checked. Each stone that was put in place was counted and they were then paid for every stone they laid. Most of the workforce were illiterate but could devise marks which singled them out from the other masons working at the castle.

The likeness of these mason marks found on the stonework at Aigues Mortes is remarkable. It suggests that some of those masons who built Aigues Mortes also worked on Flint Castle.

The castle is quite unique for the numbera nd variety of its masons' marks which can easily be found on the stone work. The best places to find them are in the inner moat on the wall near to the inner drawbridge, on the Donjon Tower base and also inside on the upper floor levels. The masons' marks are preserved because these areas have not been exposed to the weather like some of the outer walls. See how many you can find - there are over 42 marks to be found!

The O shaped ones in the basement of the North East Tower were the mark of John White, a London mason who was an expert of his time at doing concave stonework. He also dressed the inner well with stone and you can also find his marks in the basement of the Donjon Tower.

Left page: assorted masons' marks at Flint Castle

Above left: Arrow mark

Below left: O mark of John White

Chapter 5

The Development of Flint Town

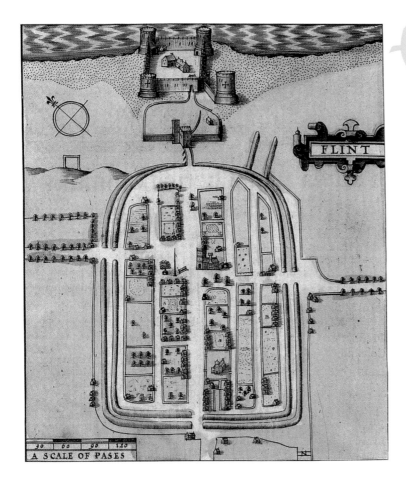

John Speed's map, 1610 (courtesy of the National Library of Wales)

Edward also built a town alongside the castle. Its first occupants included some of the English builders who chose to remain after the castle was completed. By February 1278, the first burgage plots were being granted for the new town and by 1292, there were 74 burgesses (settlers) who were wealthly enough to be taxed. The settlers included the king's tailor who had been responsible for some of the provisioning of the royal forces and several of the castle's master builders. The local Welsh were not permitted to become burgesses.

The new town originally had seventy-eight houses constructed in wood, built within the stockade that was protected by a double ditch. It was a bastide town, (bastide is the medieval word for a new town planted in open country) and was laid out to a grid pattern, a series of straight streets crossing one another at right angles.

John Speed, a renowned 17th century map-maker, drew a detailed map of Flint in 1610. His map clearly shows the grid pattern of the town and the clear links with the castle, also the outer bailey and gatehouse of the castle.

His map clearly shows that, even by 1610, over 300 years after the town was originally built, very few houses had been built outside the original town. The population probably preferred to remain close to the castle, within the safety of the stockade.

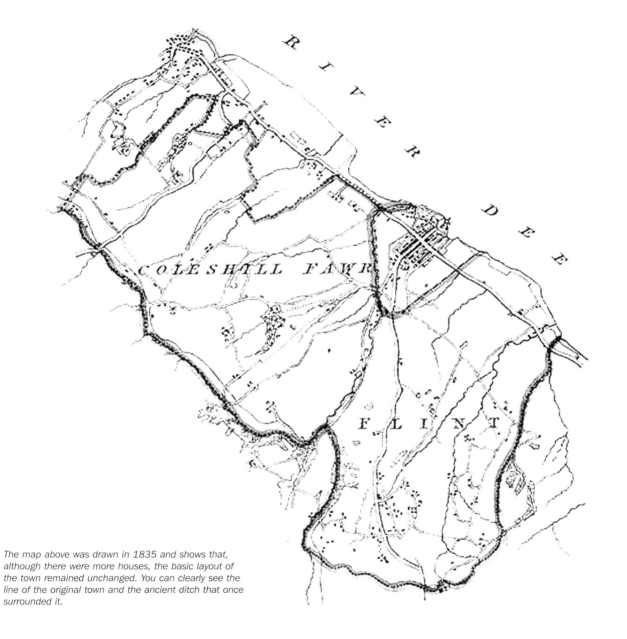

The map above was drawn in 1835 and shows that, although there were more houses, the basic layout of the town remained unchanged. You can clearly see the line of the original town and the ancient ditch that once surrounded it.

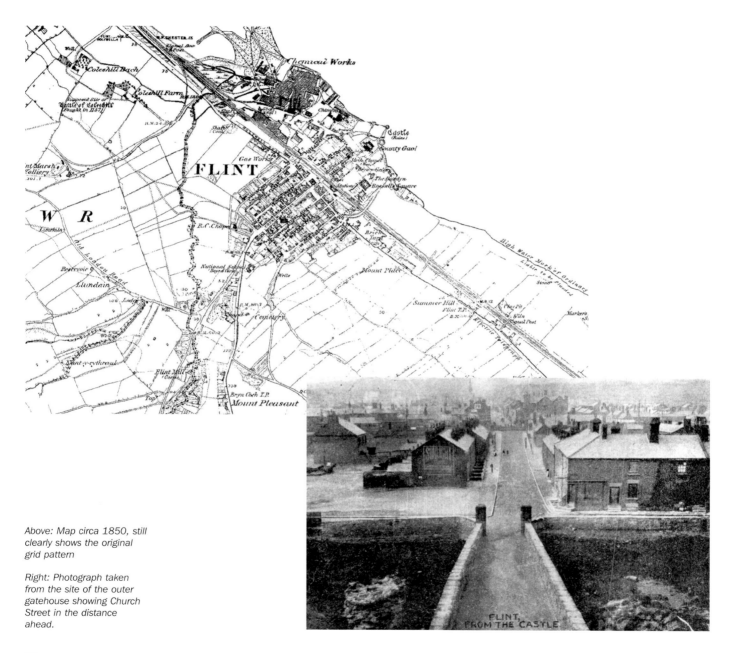

Above: Map circa 1850, still clearly shows the original grid pattern

Right: Photograph taken from the site of the outer gatehouse showing Church Street in the distance ahead.

This photograph taken in 1936 still clearly shows the shows the original grid pattern

The modern town has greatly expanded and no longer follows the original grid pattern. The grid was altered when the railway was built in 1848, then further modified when the high-rise flats, Bolingbroke and Richard Heights, were built in 1969, and when road systems were changed to meet the needs of modern traffic. However, remnants of the original grid pattern still remain.

If you stand at the site of the the outer gatehouse of the castle and look towards the town, you will find that you are looking straight up Church Street. The rows of houses in the immediate vicinity of the castle were built along the original grid pattern.

Flint's Charters

In September 1284, Edward I paid a visit to the near completed castle to bestow a Royal Charter on the town. The town was already of some importance, holding the Great County court four times a year but this first charter was quite significant because it made flint a Free Borough and confirmed a grant made in 1278 (dated at Dover on 4th February) for the provision of a market and fayre to be held in the town. Edward also granted charters to Caernarfon and Rhuddlan, signed and dated at Flint Castle, thus making Flint the birthplace of municipal government in Wales.

The first Constable of the Castle after the granting of the first charter was Reginald de Grey. He had been one of Edward's commanders in the fight against Llywelyn ap Grufydd and was highly thought of by Edward, who had also given him the Lordship of Ruthin in 1282.

Following the establishment of the castle and town for English settlers, Edward I issued the Statute of Rhuddlan which divided North and West Wales into counties, including the county of Flint, on the English model and established an administrative and judicial system unchanged for nearly 300 years.

The early charters gave great liberties and advantages to the new inhabitants who were largely English which were denied to the Welsh. No Welshman could be a burgess or hold any civic office and they were never allowed to carry weapons or hold assemblies or to purchase property or land within the Borough. The charter also stated that those living within five leagues of the town who wished to trade were forced to bring their produce, including brewed ale, into the town to be sold, in effect creating a monopoly.

In total six royal charters were granted to Flint:

September 8th, 1284 by Edward I

1327 by Edward III

1361 by Edward the Black Prince

1395 by Richard II

1595 by Phillip and Mary

1700 by William III

Each charter confirmed the rights granted in its predecessors and gave additional rights to the town.

In 1984 Flint Castle was the venue for the celebration of the 700th anniversary of the granting of our first Charter. The event took two years to arrange and cost a total of £7000. I find this quite ironic really because that was almost the cost of the building of Flint Castle!

The event was attended by the Mayor of Flint and his Mayoress, Councillor Brendan Curtis and Mrs Mary Curtis, Lord Mostyn, Keith Raffan MP, and the Mayors of Caernarfon and Rhuddlan whose forbearers had come to Flint Castle for the granting of their first charters in 1284.

Seven thousand people came along to enjoy a day of entertainment by all groups from within the town, who had got into the spirit of the event and dressed up in costume. Local children took a leading role, performing a play inside the castle walls depicting 700 years of the town's history.

But no visitor to our castle aroused more interest amongst those coming to enjoy the day than Red Rum, winner of the Grand National on three occasions. That's me in the front of the horse carrying the Charter we had made to celebrate this occasion. It is is now on display in Flint Town Hall.

Chapter 6

Major events associated with the Castle

Many interesting events have taken place around the ancient castle walls over the centuries, from the granting of the first charter, to its continued use today for major events and celebrations in the town.

In 1294 Flint town was raised in self-inflicted flames. The houses were burnt on the orders of the Constable of the Castle, William de la Leye, to defend the castle from attack by the Welsh. This desperate act of sacrificing the town to protect the castle, was to prevent the Welsh gaining shelter within the town or stealing the provisions contained there. All the 78 houses were raised to the ground. 75 burgesses put in claims for compensation for loss of buildings and goods at the time[17].

In 1304, repair work was carried out to the castle after a bad storm had blown the wooden tiles off the roof of the great hall on the outer bailey. 1200 new wooden tiles were required. At the same time a wooden gallery was added to the Donjon Tower and an ornate wooden chest. The total cost of this work was £25.00d.

The following extract from a Flint Plea Roll (requests to the king for payment like a modern bill) gives useful information on the damage, who did the repairs, and details of the castle's structure. Once again, Richard L'Engenour was in charge of the work. A wooden chamber was also added between

---

[17] *See Welsh Roll of 6 Edward I., memb xi.*

the Donjon Tower and the inner bailey for extra security as the sea was receding making the castle more vulnerable to attack.

To Roger de Mellele and William his son, carpenters repairing the bretasche (outer wall) of Flint Castle towards Coleshulle, by a tempest much damage in the walls and other places; and likewise covering of the Hall, Kitchen and Granary by the same tempest damaged, for their wages from the 23rd day of February up to the 14th day of March. To James del Wode, porter, servant to the aforesaid carpenters, and carrying Shingles upon the Hall and Kitchen for his wages during the said three weeks, namely 18 working days, by the day 1½d.

To William Faber for working of two pieces of Ewelowe iron for the door of the afore-said bretasche towards Colshulle, and 18 pieces of Ewelowe iron for the windows in the Chapel of the Great Tower and the window of the chamber next to the said chapel, for every piece 1½d.

To Walter Cordy, carpenter, making wooden chamber beyond the new bridge between the Great Tower and the inner bailey of the aforesaid castle, by order of the justice and Richard L'Engenour. For 600 great nails, called 'spikings ' bought for the said chamber 15d.

To Thomas the Carpenter and his fellow wood cutters for cutting 10,000 shingles in Ewelowe Wood for the Kitchen and Stable, for every 1000 4d. To Gilbert le Sagher for cutting 2000 shingles for the covering of the same houses 8s.

Piers Gaveston and Edward I

The only recorded visit to Flint Castle by Edward II was to meet his haughty favourite Piers Gaveston in 1311.

Piers Gaveston was born in Gascon, son of Arnaud de Gabaston, a Gascon Knight who was in the service of Gascon VII of Bearn. Through this service his father came into a substantial amount of land in Gascony and his marriage to Claramonde de Marsan.

Piers had originally made a good impression on Edward I who assigned him to the household of his son, Prince Edward of Caernarvon. They soon became very close and it was alleged that Edward and Piers became lovers (although Piers did marry and sired four children). Edward I disapproved of the relationship developing between the young men and sent Piers into exile.

After Edward I died in July 1307, his son, now Edward II, recalled Gaveston and made him the first Earl of Cornwall on 6th August 1307. This reflects his influence on Edward II as the position would traditionally been reserved for minor royals. This Earldom gave Gaveston substantial lands over a great part of England, consisting of most of Cornwall, parts of Devonshire and Berkshire, valued at £4,000 per year.

Edward also arranged for him to marry Margaret de Clare, sister of the powerful Earl of Gloucester. His association with Edward II remained strong, but their relationship fell foul of the immerging new-found concerns about sexual morals, and there was concern amongst the nobility over the control that Gaveston had over King Edward.

At Warwick, Piers was captured and condemned to death by the Duke of Lancaster, without trial. He was taken out on the road towards Kenilworth, as far as Blacklow Hill, where two Welsh men ran him through before beheading him on June 19th 1312. After this deed was done Gaveston's body was just left at the side of the road but eventually a group of Dominican friars brought it to Oxford. The King had him buried in an elaborate ceremony at Langley and a cross was erected at Blacklow Hill at the place believed to be the location of Gaveston's execution.

Below: Cartoon based on one in the Comic History of England 1847-48

The deposing of Richard II

The most important event to happen within the ancient walls of the castle must be the deposing of Richard II in August 1399, for this was a monumental event in English history. Richard had undertaken an expedition to Ireland to avenge the death of Roger Mortimer, Earl of March, and Lord Lieutenant of Ireland, who had been slain by rebel forces. Henry Bolingbroke, the King's cousin, took advantage of the King's absence to return from banishment, landing in England in July 1399. Richard received this news whilst in Ireland and returned to the country in September, landing at Haverfordwest and making his way with haste to Conwy Castle, hoping to muster support from his loyal Welsh supporters. Reputedly Richard travelled dressed as a monk so as not to be recognised.

He had only been there a few days when Sir Percy, Earl of Northumberland joined the King and his party. Percy informed the King that Bolingbroke was back in the country seeking an interview for two purposes. Firstly a patriotic one, asking that the nation be allowed the privilege of having a parliament, and secondly, a personal one, the restoration

Left: Illustration of the meeting of Richard II and Bolingbroke at Flint Castle by Randolph Caldscott, 1883. It shows Henry Bolingbroke who had 'taken his cap off to the King in an elaborate gesture', Richard in monk's attire and Richard's dog Mathe makes a fuss of Henry.

of his alienated property. The King mistrusted Sir Percy, so to convince the King of his sincerity Percy accompanied Richard to High Mass in the chapel of Conwy Castle, where he took an oath of allegiance to the King by placing his sword on the altar. The snare was laid; this act of betrayal convinced the King that Percy was sincere.

Richard decided to leave the relative safety of Conwy Castle, but had only travelled a few miles when, in the distance, he could see an army approaching headed by a military band bearing the standard of the Earl of Northumberland. At a point near Penmaen Rhos, Richard tried to escape, but to no avail as Percy sprung forward catching the bridle of the King's horse, and Richard was captured.

Firstly he was taken to Rhuddlan Castle, from where outriders were sent to Flint Castle to prepare it for the arrival of the captured monarch, and to Chester where Bolingbroke was awaiting news. Richard was moved to Flint and stayed in the Donjon Tower. When Bolingbroke heard of the King's capture, he immediately departed for Flint.

A primary account of the deposition of Richard by his cousin, Bolingbroke, can be found in an Illuminated manuscript in the British Museum (Harl. MSS.1319). The deposition was witnessed by Jean Creton, a young French nobleman who had come to England in the spring of 1399, to accompany the King to Ireland. He wrote a detailed account of the events so we know exactly what happened.

And it was enfourmed me, Kynge Richard had a grayhounde called Mathe, who always wayted upon the kynge, and wolde knowe no man els. For when so ever the kynge dyd ryde, he that kept the greyhounde dyd lette hym lose, and he wolde streyght runne to the kynge and fawne upon him, and leape upon the kynge's shoulders. And as the kynge and the erle of Derby talked togyder in the courte the grayhounde who was wont to leape upon the kynge, left the kynge and came to the erle of Derby, and made to hym the same friendly continence and chere, as he wonte to do to the kynge. The duke who knowe not the greyhounde, demanded of the kynge what the grayhounde wolde do. Cosyn, quod the kynge, it is a great good token to you and an evyil sygne to me. Sir howe knowe you that? quod the duke. I knowe it well, quod the kynge. The grayhounde maketh you chere this day as kynge of Englande as ye shalbe and I shalbe deposed; the grayhounde hathe this knowledge naturallye, therefore take him to you; he will folowe you and forsake mee. The duke understoode well those wordes, and cherished the greyhounde, who wolde never after folowe the kynge.

Jean Creton's account, complied by the historian Froissart

I find it ironic that Flint Castle was built to bring the Welsh under English rule but, just over a hundred years of it being built, it was the scene of the deposition of an English King.

Richard II

Richard was born January 6th 1367 at Bordeaux France, born into the house of Plantagenets, son of Edward the Black Prince, and Joan of Kent. At the age of 10, he ascended to the throne on June 22nd 1377 and was crowned at Westminster Abbey July 16th 1377. He married Anne of Bohemia on January 20th 1382 at the age of fifteen. When she died on 7th June 1394 he was distraught. In 1396 he married Isabella, the daughter of Charles VI of France, who was at that time only seven years of age.

In 1381, aged only thirteen, Richard was faced with the Peasants' Revolt, a result of the imposition of the Poll Tax in 1380. The leader of the Revolt, Wat Tyler, was stabbed and killed at Smithfield by the Lord Mayor of London. Richard's apparent courage in facing the mobs gathered at Mile End and Smithfield also contributed to the failure of the uprising.

His fondness for favourites resulted in conflicts with Parliament, and in 1388 the baronial party, headed by the Duke of Gloucester, had many of his friends executed. Richard recovered control in 1389, and ruled moderately until 1397, when he assumed absolute power having had the Duke of Gloucester murdered and his other leading opponents executed or banished. His cousin, Henry Bolingbroke, Duke of Hereford, returned from exile to lead a revolt. Richard II was deposed by Parliament in 1399 and imprisoned in Pontefract Castle. Here he died in mysterious circumstances at the age of 33 on February 14th, 1400 at Pontefract Castle, Yorkshire. He may have starved to death. He was originally buried at Langley but reburied at Westminster.

Above: Richard II at Flint Castle, where he was delivered prisoner to Bolingbroke, his rival to the throne. Richard is dressed in monk's attire with his hand in his pocket and Bolingbroke appears cap in hand before him. Copy of an illuminated manuscript in the British Museum

Henry Bolingbroke (Henry IV)

Henry IV, formerly Henry Bolingbroke, was born at Bolingbroke Lincolnshire on 3rd April 1367, son of John of Gaunt and Blanche of Lancaster. He married Mary Bohun in 1380, and they had seven children before her death in 1394. Mary and Henry had four sons: his successor Henry V, Thomas Duke of Clarence, John Duke of Bedford and Humphrey Duke of Gloucester, also two daughters, Blanche, who married Louis III, elector palatine of the Rhine, and Philippa, who married Eric XIII, King of Sweden. Henry's second wife was Joan, or Joanna, (c.1370-1437), daughter of Charles the Bad, King of Navarre, and widow of John IV or V, Duke of Brittany, who survived until July 1437. They had no children.

Henry had a mixed relationship with his cousin, Richard II, sometimes friendly sometimes hostile. He was one of the Lords Appellant who, in 1388, persecuted many of Richard's advisor-favourites, but his excellence as a soldier regained the King's favour and Henry was created Duke of Hereford in 1397. In 1398, however, the increasingly suspicious Richard banished him for ten years. Henry returned to England while Richard was on campaign in Ireland, leading a rebellion and usurping the throne from Richard.

As a young man Henry had been chivalrous and adventurous, and in politics anxious for good government and justice. As King he could be cruel, as demonstrated by his persecution of the Lollards, a religious group who were critical of the traditional church. He passed the burning of heretics statute in 1401 and oppression of the Lollards continued throughout his reign.

Overall Henry may be credited for maintaining his principles as a constitutional ruler. So after all his troubles he founded his dynasty firmly, and passed on a more stable crown to his son. He died in 1413 and is buried in a fine tomb in Canterbury Cathedral.

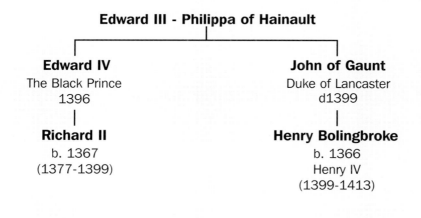

Edward III - Philippa of Hainault

Edward IV	**John of Gaunt**
The Black Prince	Duke of Lancaster
1396	d1399
Richard II	**Henry Bolingbroke**
b. 1367	b. 1366
(1377-1399)	Henry IV
	(1399-1413)

Table left: The genealogical tree shows how the royal line of accession was altered by Richard's deposition.

This painting of Richard II hangs in Westminster Hall. It is one of the oldest paintings of an English king. Painted on three panels of oak. The only copy hangs in the Council Chamber at Flint Town Hall, painted by Thomas Leonard Hughes in 1886. Hughes was born in 1862 at Greenfield, Holywell. He became an esteemed portrait painter with a studio in Bridge Street, Chester. He also painted other works such as 'Myfanwy' for which he won a gold medal at the National Eisteddfod.

This black and white reproduction doesn't do justice to the original. If you would like to see the magnifcent Hughes painting you can call at Flint Town Hall (open Monday to Friday between 10am and noon) and ask to have a look in the Council Chamber. Many other interesting portraits of local figures hang there, including Sir Roger Mostyn and Henry Taylor, along with a fascinating collection of etchings, maps and other images, relevant to Flint and its history.

Shakespeare's Richard II

William Shakespeare featured the deposition of Richard at Flint Castle in his play, 'Richard II', which reflects its significance in English history.

> *Act II scene III:*
> *Narrator: Let's talk of graves of worms and epitaphs; Make dust our paper and with rainy eyes write sorrow on the bosom of the earth. Let's choose executors and talk of wills......*
>
> *For God's sake, let us sit upon the ground, and tell sad stories of the death of Kings: How some have been deposed; some slain in war; Some haunted by the ghosts they have deposed; Some poison'd by their wives; some sleeping killed, all murdered:*
>
> *For within the hollow crown that rounds the mortal temple of a king keeps death his court.*
>
> *Go to Flint Castle: there I'll pine away a king's woe's slave shall kingly woe obey...*
>
> **Bolingbroke:** *Noble lords go to the rude ribs of that ancient castle, through brazen trumpet send the breath of parley. Into his ruined ears and thus deliver.*
>
> *In the base court where Kings grow base.[18]*

In 1899, a special performance of the play was put on in Flint Castle to commemorate the 500th anniversary of the deposition. It

[18] *William Shakespeare - Richard II, edited by Nigel Dodd MA B.MUS, Nelson & Son, 1969*

was organised by Henry Taylor, Town Clerk to Flint and the great local historian of his day.

The performance took place in front of the North East Tower on Monday August 21st 1899. It must have been the pinnacle of Henry Taylor's long career and association with Flint as it was very well attended.

Special trains were laid on to bring people to Flint to watch the performance. Reserved seats were 5s and 3s, second class seats 2s and standing room 1s.

The following is a write up about the play from the local paper.

> *Richard II Quincentenary Celebration Performance of Shakespeare's Play*
>
> *A Brilliant Gathering.....*
>
> *Within what Bolingbroke styled the "rude ribs" of the ancient Castle of Flint there was on Monday last a unique and memorable gathering – one which will be long remembered, not only by the townspeople, but also by the large army of visitors who made a peaceful invasion for the time being of the ordinarily quiet little town which disputes with Mold the honour of being regarded as the county town of the smallest of our Welsh counties.*
>
> *It was recollected that some months ago a member of the Town Council reminded his colleagues that five hundred years had elapsed since the Second Richard surrendered his kingly dignity to his cousin*

Bolingbroke within the walls of Flint Castle. The precise date of this historic incident was August 19th 1399, and the Town Council at once set about preparations with the view of celebrating it in a fitting manner. A committee was appointed to take the matter into consideration, and after various proposals had been put forward, it was finally decided to seek Mr. FR. Benson, the well-known Shakespearean actor, to give an al fresco performance of "Richard II" within the castle walls. Mr. Benson readily fell in with the views and wishes of the committee, and the result was the phenomenally successful gathering, which took place on the castle green on Monday afternoon.

FLINT CASTLE,
N. WALES.

CELEBRATION

Of the Quincentenary of the Surrender of King Richard the Second to the Earl of Bolingbroke, August 21st, 1399.

Under the Patronage of—His Grace the Duke of Westminster, Right Hon. Lord and Lady Mostyn, P. P. Pennant, Esq. (Constable of Flint Castle), &c., &c.

MONDAY, AUGUST 21st, 1899.

Arrangements have been made by a local Committee, including the Mayor and Corporation of Flint, with

MR. F. R. BENSON
AND HIS
SHAKESPEARIAN COMPANY

To give in the

GROUNDS OF FLINT CASTLE,

An *al fresco* Representation of various Scenes from Shakespeare's Play of

KING RICHARD THE SECOND,

Including the Scene of the Surrender of King Richard to the Earl of Bolingbroke, which

ACTUALLY TOOK PLACE IN FLINT CASTLE,

Five Hundred Years ago, August 21st, 1399.

A large Stage will be erected for the Performance in front of one of the Towers of the Castle, with the Sea and Mountains beyond as a natural background.

The Performance will commence at 3.30 ; Gates open at 3.

Should the weather be unfavourable the Performance will be given in a large Marquee in the Castle Grounds.

Special Trains at Reduced Fares will be run from Chester and Llandudno and Intermediate Stations

PRICES OF ADMISSION :—Reserved Stalls 5s. and 3s. ; Second Seats, 2s. ; Promeuade (no Seats), 1s.

Seats can be Booked at the North and South Wales Bank, Ltd., Flint, or will be forwarded upon receipt of Cheque or Post Office Order, addressed to Mr. E. THOMAS.

Hon Secretary :—
HENRY TAYLOR, F.S.A.,
TOWN CLERK,
TOWN HALL, FLINT.

1399.   **Flint Castle.**   1899.

The Quincentenary of the surrender of King Richard the Second to Bolingbroke on August 21st, 1399, in Flint Castle.

Under the Patronage of
His Grace the Duke of Westminster
Right Honourable Lord and Lady Mostyn.
P. P. Pennant, Esq., (Constable of Flint Castle),
&c. &c.

Programme
of the
Commemoration Performance
by

Mr. F. R. Benson's
Shakespearian Company
of
Scenes from Shakespeare's Tragedy
of
King Richard II.

August 21st, 1899.

Below: MR F R Benson

Left: Adverts for the event

Far left: The performance at Flint Castle

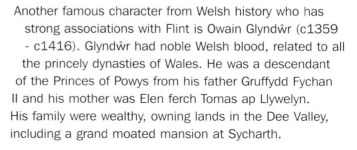

Owain Glyndŵr's rebellion

Statue of Owain Glyndwr at Corwen by sculptor, Colin Spofforth

Another famous character from Welsh history who has strong associations with Flint is Owain Glyndŵr (c1359 - c1416). Glyndŵr had noble Welsh blood, related to all the princely dynasties of Wales. He was a descendant of the Princes of Powys from his father Gruffydd Fychan II and his mother was Elen ferch Tomas ap Llywelyn. His family were wealthy, owning lands in the Dee Valley, including a grand moated mansion at Sycharth.

Although his roots were firmly planted in Wales, Owain was educated in London, studying law at the Inns of the Court. He became a loyal and distinguished soldier serving Richard II, accompanying him to Ireland as his standard-bearer.

Understandably there was no affinity between Glyndŵr and Henry Bolingbroke. Glyndŵr was in dispute with Henry's favourite, Reginald de Grey over common land that de Grey had stolen. Richard had found in favour of Glyndŵr but Henry overturned the decision. The final straw came when De Grey deliberately omitted to tell Glyndŵr that he had been summoned to provide troops for the war in Scotland, making him a traitor to King Henry who confiscated his lands. In retribution, on 16th September 1400, Glyndŵr and his supporters attacked Ruthin, burning most of the town.

The rebellion grew rapidly. There was already serious discontent amongst the Welsh, who had suffered years of oppression from successive English rulers, and men from across Wales flocked to join Glyndŵr. Almost every town in north-east Wales was attacked, including Flint.

King Henry despatched troops and rapidly drew up a range of severely punitive laws against the

Welsh, even outlawing Welsh-language bards and singers, but support for the rebellion continued to grow with higher ranking Welsh nobility joining the cause.

Among the leaders of the rebellion in Flintshire was Ithel ap Iorwerth ap Tudor of Nannerch and Howel ap Tudur of Mostyn, who was the ancestor of the present Lord Mostyn. Another of Glyndŵr's leaders Howel Gwynedd, the great-grandson of Ithel Fychan of Halkyn, carried out constant raids on the borough of Flint.

Flint was attacked once again in 1403, when the castle was beseiged and the town plundered and all but destroyed. The English burgesses of the town had to withdraw into the relative safety of the castle. The normal garrison for the castle was only 2 men-at-arms and 8 archers, but in 1403 it was increased to 120 men!

In 1404 Owain Glyndŵr was crowned King of Wales and set up a Welsh Parliament in Machynlleth. However, Henry was determined to crush the rebellion and his armies continued to fiercely campaign against the Welsh. In 1408 Aberystwyth and Harlech castles were taken and Glyndŵr's family were taken prisoner. He was forced to flee into the mountains and the rebellion was effectively over, although Glyndŵr and a few of his men continued to fight as outlaws into 1409.

Owain Glyndŵr was the last native Welshman

to hold the title Prince of Wales and he has remained a notable figure in popular culture of both Wales and England. He is portrayed in Shakespeare's play Henry IV Part I.

In the play he is described as,

'not in the roll of common men'

'a man who was wild and exotic ruled by magic and emotion. At my nativity, the front of heaven was full of fiery shapes. Of burning cressents, and at my birth the frame and high foundation of the earth shaked like a coward'

He was obviously a charismatic figure and the wording suggests that there there might have been a comet at the time of his birth, which was considered very auspicious.

Flint Castle in the Civil War

The next time that Flint Castle saw conflict, was during the Civil War between the Parliamentarians, under Oliver Cromwell, and Royalists, under Charles I.

On March 27th 1625, Charles I succeeded to the throne on the death of his father. He believed fervently in the Divine Right of Kings and throughout his reign fought with Parliament over money and religion. His marriage to Henrietta Maria, a devout Catholic who was the youngest daughter of the French king, didn't help his popularity as it was feared that he would favour and promote Catholicism.

He made constant demands to Parliament for money to fund the wars in Europe but Parliament responded coldly to his proposals, only voting small sums each time. Charles had lent ships to Louis XIII for use against the Protestants at La Rochelle, but Parliament had not been aware of Charles's intentions for the use of these ships and was greatly angered. The King's appointment of Wiilliam Laud as Archbishop of Canterbury caused further ill-feeling as his taste for priest's robes, statues and stained glass windows smacked of Catholicism. His attempt to introduce the English Prayer Book into Presbyterian Scotland caused riots. Charles also continued to favour the Duke of Buckingham whom Parliament mistrusted.

[19]*P.R.O. State Papers. Dom. 23/209.*

By 1642 the relationship between the King and Parliament had broken down completely and the country was thrown into Civil War. North Wales remained predominantly loyal to the King. Flint became involved in the conflict when Roger Mostyn was one of the first local landowners to take up arms for the King. He was just 19 years of age and was made a captain but within a few months had risen to the rank of colonel.

Mostyn repaired and garrisoned Flint Castle and raised an army at his own expense, consisting mostly of agricultural workers, miners and labourers. He was able to command the support of over 1500 men and it is estimated that the conflict cost him £60,000. After the war he was fined £825 'For taking up arms for the King' but, following the restoration of Charles II to the throne in 1660, he was rewarded and made a baronet.

Flint was influential in the war because of its strategic position, just one day's march from the garrison at Chester and also able to be supplied by boat along the River Dee, via nearby Flint Dock. Supplies of arms and ammunition could be stored at the castle and it was a useful base from which to harry the beseigers of Chester and to help blockade runners get supplies into the city by water. Flint was described as 'The King's owne castle', by Trooper Richard Symonds.[19]

The castle was the site of fierce fighting and changed hands several times during the course of the war. By the end of the war it was once again in royalist hands under the command of Roger Mostyn. It was besieged on 1st June 1646 and held out for almost three months until, having been reduced to the point of eating some of their horses to stay alive, they surrendered to Major General Thomas Mytton on 20th August 1646.

Mytton was so in admiration of their bravery that he allowed Mostyn and his men to leave under honourable terms, with banners flying and drums beating. To prove they had not been defeated they broke the flintlocks off their muskets and were allowed to walk out proud carrying their muskets over their shoulders. The present Lord Mostyn still has some of those muskets over his fireplace in the great hall at Mostyn Hall. They were allowed to return to their own homes on oath that they would not take part in any future uprising.

After the surrender Cromwell ordered that the castle be slighted (damaged irreparably), taking out the floors and blowing up stone walls so that it could never be garrisoned and used for military purposes again. The outer gate tower was also blown up and only a small amount of stone work remains to indicate where it once existed.

From this point the castle fell into decline, never to recover to its once former glory.

Above: Sir Roger Mostyn. This portrait hangs in the council chamber at Flint Town Hall and was painted by Leonard Hughes.

Above: Artist's impression of Flint Castle after it had been slighted by Parliamentarian forces (Chris Hull)

Townsfolk were encouraged to take stone from the castle for their own buildings. By 1652, the castle was described as, *'almost buried in its own ruins'*.

The town itself also suffered badly during the Civil War and was left in a poor state from which it did not recover for many years. The Parish Church had been spoiled and desecrated and the streets were silent and seemingly deserted.

John Taylor, the Water Poet, wrote in the summer of 1652,

> *They have no saddler, taylor, weaver, baker, butcher, brewer or button-maker. They have not so much as the signe of an ale-house, so that I was doubtful of a lodging. The town was devoid of industry or accommodation, scarred and stunned by the misfortunes which had befallen it.*[20]

[20]*Gleanings in North Wales – H.L. Louis - 1854*

Articles of Surrender

Articles concluded and agreed upon the 20th day of August 1646 betwixt Major Generall Mytton on ye one parte & Colonell Roger Mostyn on the other party for surrender of fflynt castle as followeth by ye commissioners undernamed:

1)   That the Governor and his servants & all commission officers and gentlemen in ye castle with their horses and armes shall have liberty to march forth to their owne homes takinge alonge with them their goods & property to them belonginge & to have permission to remayne there for six moneths next ensuinge ye date hereof without molestation in which time they may endeavour to make their peace with ye parliament or if they desire to have passes to goe beyond seas they actinge nothing in ye meane time prejudiciall unto ye state.

2)   That all common souldiers shall likewise march out with their armes, collers flyinge, drums beatinge, match lighted att both ends with bullets in their mouths unto Mostyn and their lay downe their armes and deliver them to such as Generall Mytton shall appoint & then they to goe to their own dwellings & to live quietly without molestation and not to be questioned for any former act against the parliament so they do nothinge hereafter prejudiciall unto the parliament.

3)   That Major Generall Mytton doeth ingage himselfe to write unto the parliament & use his best and most effectuall endeavores that Colonell Mostyn

may bee admitted to make his peace and compound as those yt came in and submitted before ye first of December last and in the meane time (till ye pleasure of ye parliament bee knowne) that their bee noe further sequestration upon Colonell Mostyns estate, but ye tennants to retayne their rents in their hands & ye personall & reall estate unsequestred ye 12th of this instant August to bee put into indifferent hands duringe ye space of six moneths & that John Mostyn Esquire have ye benefit of this article.

4)   In consideration whereof ye sayd Colonell Roger Mostyn doeth ingage himselfe to surrender and deliver upp ye castle of fflint with all ordinance, armes, amunition and all other provicions whatsoever now in ye sayd castle, unharmed (except before excepted) upon Munday next by eleaven of ye clocke in ye forenoone, beinge ye 24th day of this instant August unto ye sayd Major Generall Mytton or unto whom hee shall appoint for ye use of ye parliament.

Commissioners for Major Generall Mytton:
*   William Myddleton Baronett*
*   Edwards Esquire*

Commissioners for Colonell Mostyn:
*   Major John Jones*
*   Captain Peter Williams*

I doe consent unto what my commissioners have agreed.
Roger Mostyn[21]

[21]*Bodleian Library PH/WM/190788/984*

The first tourists

By the 1800s the town had recovered from its earlier misfortunes. In 1848 the area around the castle was renowned for its bathing baths and picturesque walks as the newspaper advertisements below show. Flint was one of the first towns along the North Wales Coast to take advantage of the growing fashion for sea bathing and to recognise the value of tourism. In some ways it was the forerunner of the seaside towns we now all enjoy along our coasts.

Chester Chronicle 19th May 18 1848

SALT-WATER BATHS, FLINT

Mr. Hall respectfully informs the Public generally, that his Hot and Cold Baths, and Bathing Machines, are now in full operation, and the lowest scale of charges will be adopted, in order to ensure an extensive patronage.

We invite attention to these baths as advertised in another page. Those who, at this delightful season, would recreate themselves, and in addition to the luxury of a bath, enjoy the picturesque beauties of Welsh scenery, cannot do better than sail down the river to Mr. Hall's establishment, returning to Chester by rails. It is a cheap and healthy trip. The delightful rural walks in the vicinity of Flint are much increased in interest by extensive marine views; and since the discontinuance of the chemical works, the objection to a supposed unhealthy atmosphere is removed. We hear that the arrangements of Mr. and Mrs. Hall have afforded general satisfaction.

Nowadays it is hard for us all to comprehend what a busy area this was, with the docks busily plying visitors to and from Parkgate and Chester to come and enjoy the air on the promenade by the castle. The inclusion of sea baths near the castle greatly added to the town's attractions. Three grand three-storey houses provided accommodation for visitors who had come to partake of the 'salubrious air'.

Many people plied their trades in the area around the castle. Over forty businesses were operating in the area. The adjoining table compiled from a Rates Book of 1844, shows the range of businesses at that time.

However industrial development put paid to the growing tourist trade. By 1852 there were three chemical works near the castle, including Richard Muspratt's large factory. They were highly polluting, producing suphurous and acidic gases and pouring toxins into the sea.

DATE	NAME	BUSINESS	ADDRESS
1835	Joseph Gardener	Castle Inn	Castle View
1835	George Roskell & Co	Lead Smelters	Flint Works
1835	David Scott	Engineer, Iron Merchant, steam engine, boiler maker & Colliery agent	Flint Quay
1835	Pickering & Ormiston	Flint Marsh Colliery	Flint
1840	William Jones	Customs Officer	Castle Street
1840	Michael Parry	Timber Merchant & Boat Builder	Flint Marsh
1840	David Scott	Engineer & Smith	Flint Marsh
1840	William Whitehouse	Iron Forge	Flint Marsh
1844	Joseph Hall	Public Baths	Sea side
1844	Edward Pritchard	Flint Gaol & House of Correction	Castle Street
1844	Rev. Thomas Birch Llywellyn	Baptist Chapel	Roskell Lane
1844	John Hughes	Blacksmith	Castle View
1844	Daniel Scott	Boiler Maker	Castle View
1844	John Hughes	Boiler Maker	Evans Row
1844	R Mellor, J Lewis	Boot & Shoe Makers	Castle Street
1844	Samuel Hodgkinson	Butcher	Castle View
1844	Robert Evans	Coal Agent	Bardyn Cottage
1844	William Jones	Coal Agent	Castle View
1844	Eyton Bros	Coal Proprietors	Flint Colliery
1844	John Ormiston	Coal Proprietors	Marsh Colliery
1844	George Parry	Cooper	Castle View
1844	E Gratton, R Taylor	Corn & Flour Dealers	Castle Street
1844	Scott Daniel	Engineer	Castle Street
1844	John Blunt	Grocer & Dealer in Sundries	Castle Street
1844	H Danny, M Harris, E Lloyd	Grocers & Dealer in Sundries	Evans Row
1844	William Morris	Grocer & Dealer in Sundries	Roskell Buildings
1844	George Parry	Grocer & Dealer in Sundries	Castle View
1844	Robert Edwards	Castle Inn	Castle View
1844	J Jones, T Parry, S Porter	Retailers of Beer	Castle View
1844	Thomas Hughes	Joiner	Evans Row
1844	Peter Bibby	Joiner	Castle Street
1844	George Roskell &Co	Lead Smelters	Flint Works
1844	Mary Hall	Milliner & Dressmaker	Baths
1844	Thomas Evans	Saddles	Evans Row
1844	Richard Dawson	Surveyor	Evans Row
1844	Peter Edwards	Tailor	Castle Street
1844	John Cadwallader Jones	Timber Dealer	Flint Quay
1844		Billiard Room	Castle Street
1844	William Evans	Relieving Officer Docks	Castle View
1844	William Whitehouse	Iron Forge	Flint Quay
1844	E Bithell, E Foulkes, J Price	Conveyors by water	Flint Quay

Fishing

Fishing has been a part of Flint life for centuries, with the Dee Estuary providing a valuable source of food. Until the 1950s a row of old fishermen's cottages stood alongside the castle. The ruined castle has been painted by numerous artists, most notably by J.M. Turner. Almost every painting and etching includes fishermen and fishing boats, reflecting the role that fishing played in the local economy.

The chemical pollution of the late 1800s hit the fishing industry hard. However, since the factories closed, stocks of fish and shellfish have recovered well. Once again commercial fishermen work on the estuary, cockle fishing in the summer and landing seasonal catches, including bass, flounder and shrimp, throughout the year. Numerous anglers also fish for pleasure.

The best known Flint fishermen were the Bithell family who fished on the Dee for generations. They held valuable salmon fishing licences and also ran a fishmongers near the castle.

Left: Flint Castle, by J.M. Turner, 1830s (a copy is on show in Flint Town Hall)

Left: Flint Castle, showing the fishermen's cottages in the foreground, circa mid 1800s

Below: Two other paintings hanging in Flint Town Hall that reflect the fishing heritage

The Crimea War Cannon

Flint has always recognised international events. This led the Borough Council to petition the government for a token to commemorate the Crimean War.

Flintshire Observer 24th December 1857

BOROUGH OF FLINT
The Town Clerk of this Borough having applied to the Hon. Lord Panmure, Secretary of State for War, for a Russian gun, or other trophy, as a memorial of the late Crimean War, has received the following letter from Sir John Ramsden, Bart., the Under Secretary:-

WAR OFFICE, 14TH DEC., 1857

Sir, I am directed by Lord Panmure to inform you, that his lordship has much pleasure in presenting to the Borough of Flint one Russian iron gun, as a trophy of the late war, for the correct mounting and careful preservation of which his lordship feels confident that he may rely on the public spirit of the inhabitants of the place.

As there is not at his lordship's disposal any carriage to accompany the gun, I am directed to transmit to you the enclosed lithographs of three kinds of Russian gun carriage, and to state that in the event of the authorities of Flint being desirous of having a carriage constructed after any one of these patterns, and undertaking to repay the expense, his lordship is prepared to authorize its manufacture at the Royal Arsenal, Woolwich.

I am, Sir, Your obedient Servant
J. N. RAMSDEN.

The Council agreed to fund a gun carriage and the cannon was duly delivered. This account of the gun's inaugauration gives the flavour of the event.

Flintshire Observer 1st October 1858
The inauguration of the Russian gun, presented by the Government to the Corporation, took place on the anniversary of the battle of Alma, amid great manifestations of popular enthusiasm. The gun had been beautifully lacquered by Mr Robert Williams, Painter, and placed upon a handsome iron carriage, the gift of Mr Astbury, of Rockcliff, and altogether it looked extremely well, and will form an interesting ornament to the ancient ruins of the castle.

At about noon a procession was formed at the Guild Hall and headed by the band of the Royal Flint Rifles, the gun was taken down in triumph drawn by three splendid cart horses from Messrs Muspratt and Huntley's Chemical Works, all decorated with ribbons. The gentlemen of the committee who had arranged the proceedings, and including Mr Joseph Evans, Mr E Williams Jones, Mr John Jones, Cross Foxes, Mr J F Edwards, and Mr Jackson, of the Castle Inn, bore banners in the procession.

The procession started from the Hall keeping time to the inspiring notes of a military march, played by the band, and after parading the main street, proceeded to the castle, where the gun was placed upon a large freestone platform, of

50335. FLINT. THE CASTLE COURTYARD.

Yorkshire flag, prepared for its reception at the expense of the Messrs Muspratt; and after it had been fixed in its position, Mr Ellis Eyton, the town clerk, standing upon the gun, addressed the assembly and, in the name of the mayor, inaugurated the gun. In conclusion, he asked for three cheers for the Queen, and cheers for the Army and Navy. Three cheers were most heartily responded to as well as three cheers for Mr Eyton, after which a royal salute of 21 guns was fired from the gun.

The town during the day was remarkably full of visitors. Business was suspended at 10.o'clock, and an infinity of amusements followed. It was estimated that several thousand were present, and that the number of persons far exceeded any assemblage ever witnessed at an election. Upward of £15 was subscribed to defray the expenses of the day, and quantities of tea and bread were given to about 100 poor families of the town and neighbourhood.

The cannon was taken away during the Second World War to be melted down for the war effort. Locals were very sad to see it go.

The Royal Welsh Fusiliers at Flint Castle

The County Gaol was built on the outer bailey of Flint Castle in 1785 and housed prisoners until it closed in 1880. It was well used by all accounts for in the 1841 census, Edward Pritchard, who was in charge of the gaol with his wife Ann and their three children, had it occupied by 18 prisoners ranging in age from 15 to 55 years old.

From 1912 to 1969, the same site was used as the headquarters of the 3rd Battalion of the Royal Welch Fusiliers. The army buildings included a large Drill Hall.

The Territorial Army Headquarters and Drill Hall closed in 1969 and the buildings were demolished.

DRILL HALL, FLINT CASTLE   218190

Above: Drill Hall

Left page:
Above: Aerial view showing the location of the drill hall.

Far left: Another view of the army buildings on the outer bailey

Below: Embroidery given by Queen Victoria to the Royal Welsh Fusliiers (on show in Flint Town Hall)

Chapter 7

The Castle today

The castle, although now in ruins with its military importance long gone, continues to be an important landmark in the town. For hundreds of years, it has been used as a venue for local celebrations and this tradition continues today.

This photograph of the Rechabite tea in 1910 shows one such event but there will undoubtedly have been used for many other events that may not have been recorded by photographers. (The Rechabites were a Friendly Society whose members had to sign a pledge to abstain from alcohol.)

In recent times, the castle has been used for numerous events, ranging from open air theatre and concerts to Medieval re-enactments, a Teddy Bear's picnic and the launch of the Wales Coast Path.

Top left: A Celtic evening at the castle

Bottom left: David Bellamy who came to support the Keep Wales Tidy Campaign.

Bottom right: A Medieval re-enactment that was part of Flint Town's Festival - an annual event for a fortnight in June and July

Exploring the area

The footpath alongside the castle is now part of the newly opened Wales Coast Path, a clearly waymarked route which follows the entire Welsh coast for over 800 miles. Why not stroll along the coast east towards Chester, or west along the North Wales coast, taking in the breathtaking views of the River Dee and marshes, watching the boats and the birdlife?

As you walk, ponder on the changing face of Flint's coast. This former military stronghold and port was a seaside resort and then a bustling industrial area. Now it is peaceful again, internationally important for its birdlife, and a refreshing place to walk.

Imagine the thousands of others who may have trodden these paths before you; the workers forcibly marched from Chester to build the castle, numerous soldiers over the centuries whether Roman, Welsh, Norman and Saxon, fishermen tending their nets, sailors whose boats had docked at the port, industrial workers walking to work or taking a break, and local people and visitors coming to enjoy the coast and Flint's rich heritage.

Birdwatching

Flint's coast is a great place for bird watching throughout the year. Ravens breed in the castle but it is the saltmarsh and mudflats that attract most species as the rich estuary mud is full of invertebrate life, providing plentiful food.

Some birds remain all year and breed locally. Some of the most common and easily recognized are shelduck, curlew, redshank, and oystercatcher.

In winter, they are joined by thousands of wading birds that migrate from the Arctic. Flocks of small waders, like dunlin and knot, scurry across the exposed mud, or, wheel into the sky when disturbed, their shrill calls breaking the silence. Many other species pass through in spring and autumn on migration between the Tropics and the Arctic. They use the estuary as a vital staging post, to rest and feed.

Top: Oystercatchers

Left: Shelduck

Below: Knot

Flint Dock

Following the footpath west along the coast, you soon come to Flint Dock. It has links with the castle, initally developing under its protection and, much later, it was reinforced with stone taken from the abandoned castle.

In the early 19th century the small port of Flint was thriving, exporting lead, coal and chemicals and importing timber, slates and other products. By 1833, Flint was the main port of Chester, as boats could no longer reach the city due to the silting of the Dee. In one year over 300 ships, including six from America, docked at the port. In 1840, it is recorded that there were 20 boats waiting to be offloaded at Flint Dock at any one time.

The main boats were Flint flats, which were built in the adjoining shipyards. As their name suggests they had flatter bottoms so that they could sail easily up the silting river.

It is now a peaceful place to walk and relax. While you are sitting and enjoying the view, think back to when it was a busy port.

In my role as Castle Custodian, I visit the castle every day and always meet someone there, whether its an elderly couple taking a stroll, young families, school groups or foreign tourists.

This happy family sitting on the curtain wall overlooking the marshland and Parkgate are typical of the summer visitors who come to both enjoy the views and picnic in the grounds of the castle. At present there is very little information at the castle to help visitors unravel its history. I hope that this book will encourage visitors, both locals and tourists alike, to take a closer look at the remains of the castle and to gain a better understanding of its importance in local and national history.

About the Author

I was born on January 3rd 1949 in the front room of my parents' (Frank & Prudy Aldridge) house, 185 Chester Road, Flint. Youngest daughter of eight children, born and brought up in Flint, I can say with pride that I am "off Flint". I am proud of living in Flint and have watched it grow over the time I have lived here. I have had the honour of serving on the Town Council and being the town Mayor. My greatest achievement has been to be the key-keeper of Flint Castle for over twenty-six years and I hope to continue in this role for many years to come.

I have already written many articles and small guide books of the town and town hall. This book is the biggest I have done so far, but is not the last one I will do as this book is part one and, as I type this, I am also working on the next one.

Courtesy of the Bodleian Library Oxford

Bibliography

Albaric, Alain, *Aigues-Mortes*

Cohen, M.J. & Major, John, *History in Quotations*, Cassell

Emerson, Christina, *Aigues-Mortes Tourist Guide*

Evans-Gunther, Charles W., *Llywelyn our Last Prince*, Clwyd County Council

Finnegan, Ruth, *Studying Family and Community History*, (Cambridge University Press).

Gerald of Wales - Gerald ac Gumro, 1188

Herbert, Dr. Trevor & Elwyn Jones, Gareth, *Edward I and Wales*, Cardiff Uni. Press 1988

Perfect, Vicky *'Flint Town Guide'*, 1999, for Flint Town Council

Perfect, Vicky *Disappearing Flint (Leaflet)*

Powicke, Sir Maurice, *The Thirteenth Century 1216-1300*, Oxford Uni. Press

Smith B, (1921), *Lead and Zinc Ores of North Wales Vol. XIX*

Prestwich, Michael, *Edward I*, Guild Publishing

Taylor, A. J., *Castle Building Thirteenth Century Wales and Savoy*, British Academy London

Taylor, A. J., *The Castles of St George de Esperanch*

Taylor, A. J., *Flint Castle A postscript*, Flintshire Historical Society Publication, 1958

Taylor, Henry, MA F.S.A. *Historic Notices of Flint, 1883*, Elliot Stock

Wrigley, E.A. *Poverty, Progress, and Population*, Cambridge University Press

Flintshire Historical Society Book, 1957

Flint Map 1870, Flintshire Record Office, Hawarden

Flint Map 1939, Flintshire Record Office, Hawarden

Slaters Directory, 1883

1881 census, Flint Library

1841 census, Church of the Latter Day Saints

Researched at and consulted:

County Library Civic Buildings Mold

Flintshire Record Office, Hawarden, Flintshire

Flint Town Library, Church Street, Flint

Flint Town Hall, Market Square, Flint

Houses of Parliament Library

House of Lords Reference Library

Bodleian Library, Oxford

Royal Historical Society, Sir Otho de Grandison 1238 - 1328